FINISH LINE

Mathematics
for the Common Core State Standards

Continental

ISBN 978-0-8454-6760-2

Table of Contents

Welcome to Finish Line Mathematics for the Common Core State Standards

About This Book

Finish Line Mathematics for the Common Core State Standards will help you prepare for math tests. Each year in math class, you learn new skills and ideas. This book focuses on the math skills and ideas that are the most important for each grade. It is important to master the concepts you learn each year because mathematical ideas and skills build on each other. The things you learn this year will help you understand and master the skills you will learn next year.

This book has units of related lessons. Each lesson concentrates on one main math idea. The lesson reviews things you have learned in math class. It provides explanations and examples. Along the side of each lesson page are reminders to help you recall what you learned in earlier grades.

After the lesson come three pages of practice problems. The problems are the same kinds you find on most math tests. The first page has multiple-choice, or selected-response, problems. Each item has four answers to choose from, and you must select the best answer. At the top of the page is a sample problem with a box beneath it that explains how to find the answer. Then there are a number of problems for you to do on your own.

Constructed-response, or short-answer, items are on the next page. You must answer these items using your own words. Usually, you will need to show your work or write an explanation of your answer in these items. This type of problem helps you demonstrate that you know how to do operations and carry out procedures. They also show that you understand the skill. Again, the first item is a sample and its answer is explained. You will complete the rest of the items by yourself.

The last page has one or two extended-response problems. These items are like the short writing items, but they have more parts and are often a little harder. The first part may ask you to solve a problem and show your work. The second may ask you to explain how you found your answer or why it is correct. This item has a hint to point you in the right direction.

At the end of each unit is a review section. The problems in it cover all the different skills and ideas in the lessons of that unit. The review contains multiple-choice, constructed-response, and extended-response items.

A practice test and a glossary appear at the end of the book. The practice test gives you a chance to try out what you've learned. You will need to use all the skills you have reviewed and practiced in the book on the practice test. The glossary lists important words and terms along with their definitions to help you remember them.

The Goals of Learning Math

Math is everywhere in the world around you. You use math more than you probably realize to help you understand and make sense of that world. But what does it mean to be good at math?

To be good at math, you need to practice certain habits. And you need the right attitude.

- You make sense of problems and do not give up in solving them. You make sure you understand the problem before you try to solve it. You form a plan and then carry out that plan to find an answer. Along the way, you ask yourself if what you are doing makes sense. And if you do not figure out the answer on the first try, you try another way.

- You think about numbers using symbols. You can think about a real-life situation as numbers and operations.

- You draw conclusions about situations and support them with proof. You use what you know about numbers and operations to provide reasons for your conclusions and predictions. When you read or hear someone else's explanation, you think about it and decide if it makes sense. You ask questions that help you better understand the ideas.

- You model with mathematics. You represent real-life problems with a drawing or diagram, a graph, or an equation. You decide if your model makes sense.

- You use the right tools at the right time. You know how to use rulers, protractors, calculators, and other tools. More importantly, you know when to use them.

- You are careful and accurate in your work. You calculate correctly and label answers. You use the correct symbols and definitions. You choose exactly the right words for your explanations and descriptions.

- You look for structure in math. You see how different parts of math are related or connected. You can use an idea you already know to help you understand a new idea. You make connections between things you have already learned and new ideas.

- You look for the patterns in math. When you see the patterns, you can find shortcuts to use that still lead you to the correct answer. You are able to decide if your shortcut worked or not.

These habits help you master new mathematical ideas so that you can remember and use them. All of these habits will make math easier to understand and to do. And that will make it a great tool to use in your everyday life!

● **Lesson 1 Whole-Number Place Value** reviews what place value is and how to use it to read and write numbers in standard form, word form, and expanded form.

● **Lesson 2 Comparing Whole Numbers** reviews how to use place value to compare and order whole numbers.

● **Lesson 3 Rounding Whole Numbers** reviews how to round whole numbers to the nearest tens, hundreds, thousands, ten thousands, and hundred thousands.

● **Lesson 4 Factors and Multiples** reviews what factors and factor pairs are and how they relate to multiplication and multiples.

● **Lesson 5 Prime and Composite Numbers** reviews what prime numbers and composite numbers are and how to find them.

Whole-Number Place Value

4.NBT.1, 4.NBT.2

The value of any place is $\frac{1}{10}$ the value of the place to its left.

To find the value of a place to the left, divide by 10.

$50,000 \div 10 = 5,000$

$5,000$ is $\frac{1}{10}$ of $50,000$.

The **word form** of a number shows the number name.

Three hundred five thousand

In expanded form, you do not need to write a product if the value of a place is 0.

Numbers in **standard form** are written with numerals.

305,000

Place value is the value of a digit depending on its position in a number. Place values are based on ten. The value of each place is ten times the value of the next place to its right.

How does the value of the 5 in the ten thousands place compare to the value of the 5 in the hundreds place?

hundred thousands	ten thousands	thousands	hundreds	tens	ones
6	5	3,	5	2	1

The value of the ten thousands place is 10,000, so the 5 has a value of $5 \times 10,000 = 50,000$.

The value of the hundreds place is 100, so the 5 has a value of $5 \times 100 = 500$.

The value of each place is 10 times greater than the place to the right. The ten thousands place is 2 places to the right of the hundreds place. Its digit is 10×10 or 100 times greater than the digit in the hundreds place.

$$500 \times (10 \times 10) = 500 \times 100 = 50,000$$

So 50,000 is 100 times greater than 500.

You can use place values to read and write numbers in expanded form. **Expanded form** shows a number as the sum of the values of its places.

What is the expanded form of 236,408?

Write each digit as a product of the digit and the value of its place. Then add the products.

Standard Form
236,408

Expanded Form
$= (2 \times 100,000) + (3 \times 10,000) +$
$(6 \times 1,000) + (4 \times 100) + (8 \times 1)$

SAMPLE What is the standard form of (3 × 10,000) + (7 × 100) + (3 × 10) + (2 × 1)?

    A 3,732   **B** 30,732   **C** 37,032   **D** 300,732

> The correct answer is B. To find the standard form of the number, first find each product in parentheses: (3 × 10,000) = 30,000, (7 × 100) = 700, (3 × 10) = 30, (2 × 1) = 2. Then add the products: 30,000 + 700 + 30 + 2 = 30,732.

1 In 5,743,029, which digit is in the hundred thousands place?

    A 5   **C** 4

    B 3   **D** 7

2 Which is the expanded form of 40,650?

    A (4 × 100,000) + (6 × 10) + (5 × 1)

    B (4 × 10,000) + (6 × 1,000) + (5 × 100)

    C (4 × 10,000) + (6 × 100) + (5 × 10)

    D (4 × 1,000) + (6 × 100) + (5 × 10)

3 There are 2,032,064 ants in one colony. What is the value of the 3 in this number?

    A 3   **C** 3,000

    B 30   **D** 30,000

4 Which digit has the greatest value in 1,789?

    A 1   **C** 8

    B 7   **D** 9

5 Which is (5 × 100,000) + (3 × 1,000) + (6 × 10) + (7 × 1) in standard form?

    A 5,367   **C** 503,067

    B 530,067   **D** 503,607

6 In which number does the 7 have the greatest value?

    A 137,806   **C** 13,786

    B 1,370,806   **D** 1,037,806

7 What is the standard form of nine million, twenty-seven thousand, four hundred three?

    A 927,403   **C** 9,207,430

    B 9,270,403   **D** 9,027,403

8 Will wrote the number 26,367. How many times greater is the 6 in the thousands place than the 6 in the tens place?

    A 10   **C** 1,000

    B 100   **D** 10,000

SAMPLE Why does the number 8,537 have a different value than 8,357?

Answer _____

The two numbers have the same digits, but the digits are in different places. In 8,537, the 5 stands for 5 hundreds, or 500, and the 3 stands for 3 tens, or 30. In 8,357, the 3 stands for 3 hundreds, or 300, and the 5 stands for 5 tens, or 50.

9 The speed of light is 186,282 miles per second. Write the place name and the value of each 8 in this number.

Answer _____

10 Look at the speed of light in problem 9. Kyra says the value of the first 8 from the left is 100 times the value of the second 8. Is she correct? Explain.

_____

_____

11 Write the number 702,500 in expanded form.

Answer _____

12 In 2009, the population of Elizabethtown, Pennsylvania, was 12,103. Write this number in words.

Answer _____

13 Ronette wrote 1,071,570 in expanded form this way:

$(1 \times 1,000,000) + (7 \times 100,000) + (1 \times 10,000) + (5 \times 100) + (7 \times 10)$

What mistake did Ronette make?

_____

_____

14 Larissa visited Great Smoky Mountains National Park last year. So did 9,044,010 other people.

Part A Write the number 9,044,010 in word form and in expanded form.

Word form _____

_____

Expanded form _____

_____

Part B There are two 4's in the number 9,044,010. Matt says the 4 on the left is 10 times the value of the 4 on the right. Missy says the 4 on the right is $\frac{1}{10}$ the value of the 4 on the left. Who is correct? Explain how you know.

Multiplying by 10 makes a number larger. Dividing by 10 makes it smaller. How is finding $\frac{1}{10}$ like dividing by 10?

_____

_____

_____

_____

_____

Comparing Whole Numbers

4.NBT.2

When you compare numbers, you determine which is larger or smaller than the other.

You can use place value to **compare** large whole numbers.

Which number is larger, 145,387 or 148,963?

Write each number vertically.   145,387
Line up the place values.   148,963

Compare the digits in the same places, starting at the left.

The hundred thousands are the same: **1**45,387
                                        148,963

The ten thousands are the same: 1**4**5,387
                                        1**4**8,963

The thousands digits are different: 14**5**,387
                                        14**8**,963

Since 5 thousands are less than 8 thousands, the larger number is 148,963. You can write this as a number sentence.

148,963 > 145,387   *or*   145,387 < 148,963

You can use place value to **order** three or more numbers.

An **inequality** is a number sentence that compares two numbers using > or <.

The symbol < means "is less than." The symbol > means "is greater than." The symbol = means "is equal to."

When you order numbers, you arrange them from greatest to least or from least to greatest.

Sports arena A has 95,672 seats. Arena B has 95,667 seats. Arena C has 95,676 seats. Order the arenas from least to greatest number of seats.

Compare the digits in the same places, starting on the left. The digits are the same in the ten thousands, thousands, and hundreds places.

Compare the tens digits. Two arenas have 7 in the tens place and one has a 6, and 6 is less than 7, so 95,667 is the least.

Compare the ones digits in 95,67**2** and 95,67**6**. The digits are 6 and 2, and 2 is less than 6. So 95,672 is less than 95,676.

From least to greatest, the numbers are 95,667, 95,672, and 95,676. The arenas in order of size are B, A, C.

SAMPLE Which inequality is true?

    A   6,092 < 6,029   **C**   1,003 < 1,003

    B   2,228 > 2,219   **D**   773 > 777

> The correct answer is B. To find which inequality is true, compare the digits in the same places of each pair of numbers. Choice A is not true because the 9 is not less than the 2 in the tens place. Choice C is not true because the numbers are equal. Choice D is not true because the 3 is not greater than the 7 in the ones place. Choice B is true because the 2 is greater than 1 in the tens place.

1 Which number is greater than 48,632?

    A   48,343   **C**   48,632

    B   48,619   **D**   49,421

2 An apple tree has 2,179 apples on it. A second apple tree has fewer apples on it. What could be the number of apples on the second tree?

    A   2,701   **C**   2,080

    B   2,185   **D**   3,186

3 Which list shows the numbers in order from least to greatest?

    A   3,905, 3,590, 3,095, 3,059

    B   3,095, 3,059, 3,905, 3,590

    C   3,059, 3,095, 3,590, 3,905

    D   3,059, 3,905, 3,095, 3,590

4 Which number is greater than 271,000 and less than 315,000?

    A   351,000   **C**   259,000

    B   306,000   **D**   217,000

5 Anil, Ben, and Cam collected cans for recycling. Anil collected 5,499 cans. Ben collected 4,950 cans, and Cam collected 5,601 cans. Which list shows the students in order from most cans to least cans?

    A   Anil, Ben, Cam

    B   Anil, Cam, Ben

    C   Cam, Anil, Ben

    D   Cam, Ben, Anil

6 Which inequality is true?

    A   83,410 < 84,310

    B   72,630 < 72,360

    C   53,650 > 65,350

    D   34,790 > 43,970

7 Which number makes this inequality true?

$$32,004 < \square$$

    A   30,980   **C**   32,001

    B   31,732   **D**   33,004

SAMPLE Order the numbers 7,642, 7,832, and 7,632 from greatest to least.

Answer _____

✓ Compare the digits of all three numbers. The digits in the thousands place are the same. In the hundreds place, two of the numbers have 6's and one has an 8, so 7,832 is the greatest number. Compare the tens place: 3 is less than 4, so, 7,632 < 7,642. The order from greatest to least is 7,832, 7,642, 7,632.

8 The table shows some of Earth's oldest trees and their estimated ages.

Which tree is the oldest? Explain how you know.

_____

_____

_____

Tree and Country	Age (years)
Common Yew, Wales	4,000
Cypress, Iran	4,200
Alerce, Chile	3,640
Bristlecone Pine, USA	4,841

9 Angela wants to order 62,906, 62,609, and 63,069 from least to greatest. In which places does she need to compare the digits?

Answer _____

10 Write a number sentence to compare 458,967, 458,796, and 459,976. Use <, >, or =.

Answer _____

11 Leo ordered these whole numbers from least to greatest this way:

190,064, 190,640, 190,460

Explain Leo's mistake. Then order the numbers correctly.

_____

_____

_____

12 In the table below, Kenya recorded the average sizes of different kinds of whales she read about.

WHALES

Type of Whale	Weight (pounds)
Blue	250,000
Fin	130,000
Humpback	65,000
Bowhead	125,000
Gray	70,000
Right	140,000

Part A Which whale weighs more than a fin whale but less than a blue whale?

Answer _____

Part B List the whales in order of their weights from least to greatest. Explain how you found your answer.

_____

_____

_____

_____

_____

_____

_____

Do all the weights have the same number of places? Be sure to compare the same places.

Rounding Whole Numbers

4.NBT.3

When you **round** a number, you replace it with a close number that tells about how many.

When rounding, look at **only** the first digit to the right of the place value you are rounding to. Ignore digits that are farther to the right. Replace them with 0's in the rounded number.

You can use place value to **round** large whole numbers.

The town library has 120,584 printed books and 45,162 audio books. A reporter rounds these numbers to the nearest thousand for a newspaper story. What are the rounded numbers?

To round numbers to the thousands place, look at the digit to the right of the thousands place.

PRINTED BOOKS

hundred thousands	ten thousands	thousands	hundreds ↓	tens	ones
1	2	0,	5	8	4

AUDIO BOOKS

hundred thousands	ten thousands	thousands	hundreds ↓	tens	ones
	4	5,	1	6	2

- If the digit to the right is **5 or greater,** "round up." Add 1 to the digit you are rounding to.

- If the digit to the right is **less than 5,** "round down." Do not change the digit you are rounding to.

In the number of printed books, 120,584, the digit in the thousands place is 0. The digit to the right in the hundreds place is 5. Because the digit is 5 or greater, round up. Add 1 to the thousands place and write 0's in the rest of the places to the right. The number rounds to 121,000.

In the number of audio books, 45,162, the digit to the right of the thousands place is 1. Because the digit is less than 5, round down. Do not change the 5 in the thousands place. Write 0's in the rest of the places to the right. The number of audio books rounds to 45,000.

SAMPLE What is 754,863 rounded to the ten thousands place?

　　　A 750,000　　**B** 754,000　　**C** 755,000　　**D** 760,000

> The correct answer is A. To round a number to the ten thousands place, look at the thousands digit. The thousands digit in 754,863 is 4, which is less than 5. So the number rounds down to 750,000.

1 Andy has a collection of 473 bottle caps. What is this number rounded to the nearest ten?

A	400	**C**	480
B	470	**D**	500

2 What is 2,642 rounded to the hundreds place?

A	3,000	**C**	2,600
B	2,700	**D**	2,640

3 Beatrice is rounding 45,387 to the thousands place. Which digit should she look at?

A	4	**C**	3
B	5	**D**	8

4 Which digit should you look at to round 134,068 to the ten thousands place?

A	3	**C**	6
B	4	**D**	8

5 Which of these numbers rounds down when rounding to the ten thousands place?

A	205,311	**C**	586,912
B	493,689	**D**	717,123

6 The population in a certain city was 1,096,843. What is the population rounded to the nearest hundred thousand?

A	900,000	**C**	1,100,000
B	1,000,000	**D**	1,900,000

7 In which place do you round up when the digit in the thousands place is 5 or more?

A	tens	**C**	thousands
B	hundreds	**D**	ten thousands

8 There were 18,652 geese on a lake. What is this number rounded to the ten thousands place?

A	20,000	**C**	19,000
B	19,600	**D**	18,600

9 Han rounds a number to the nearest thousand and gets 12,000. What could be the actual number?

A	12,910	**C**	11,529
B	12,522	**D**	11,497

SAMPLE Nadine rounds a number to the nearest thousand and gets 25,000. What are the smallest and largest numbers the original number can be?

Answer _____

✓   To round to the thousands place, a number can round up or down, depending on the hundreds digit. To round up to 25,000, the hundreds digit must be 5 or greater, so numbers starting with 24,500 round up to 25,000. To round down to 25,000, the hundreds digit must be 4 or less. So any number from 25,499 down rounds to 25,000. The smallest number to round to 25,000 is 24,500 and the largest is 25,499.

10 Frank rounds 846,025 to the nearest hundred thousand and to the nearest ten thousand. Which rounded number is greater? Explain.

_____

_____

11 Write two numbers that round to 4,000 when rounding to the nearest thousand. Make one greater than 4,000 and one less.

Answer _____

12 There are 9,321 leaves on a tree. Explain why the digit 3 stays the same when 9,321 is rounded to the nearest hundred.

_____

_____

13 In 639,453, which places will round up and which will round down?

_____

_____

14 The theater club puts on two shows each year, a musical and a drama. The table shows the ticket sales for each.

Show	Ticket Sales	Nearest Ten	Nearest Hundred
Musical	1,749		
Drama	1,024		
Total	2,773		

Part A Round each number to the nearest ten and to the nearest hundred. Write your answers in the table above.

Part B Which number would you use to show that the theater club had a very successful season? Explain.

_____

_____

_____

15 Mr. Kumar is interested in buying a house. He found two houses he likes priced at $233,250 and $226,500.

Part A Round each number to the nearest thousand.

Answer _____

Part B Round the original house prices to the nearest ten thousand. Which number is greater? Explain why.

_____

_____

_____

_____

To round to the ten thousands place, what place must the digit you look at be in?

Factors and Multiples

4.OA.4

A **factor** is a whole number that can be multiplied by another whole number to find a product. A **factor pair** is any two whole numbers that are multiplied to get a product.

Marta bakes 24 fish cakes. She puts them into different groups of equal size. What equal-sized groups can she make?

To find the groups, find the factor pairs that multiply to 24.

oooooooooooooooooooooooo $1 \times 24 = 24$

$4 \times 6 = 24$ $3 \times 8 = 24$

$12 \times 2 = 24$

Factors of 24: 1, 2, 3, 4, 6, 8, 12, 24
Factor pairs of 24: 1 and 24, 2 and 12, 3 and 8, 4 and 6

Marta can make 1 group of 24 or 24 groups of 1. She can make 2 groups of 12 or 12 groups of 2. She can make 3 groups of 8 or 8 groups of 3. She can make 4 groups of 6 or 6 groups of 4.

A **multiple** of a number is the product of a whole number and any other whole number, except zero.

Multiples of 3 are 3, 6, 9, 12, 15, 18, 21, 24, …
Multiples of 5 are 5, 10, 15, 20, 25, …

A recycling truck picks up bottles and newspapers every 4 days beginning on the 4th of each month. On which days can recyclables be put out during a month of 30 days?

Find the multiples of 4 until you get to 30 to find the days on which recyclables can be put out.

Multiples of 4: 4, 8, 12, 16, 20, 24, 28

Recyclables can be put out on the 4th, 8th, 12th, 16th, 20th, 24th, and 28th.

SAMPLE Which group shows all the factors of 12?

A 2, 3, 4, 6, 9

C 1, 2, 3, 4, 6, 12

B 2, 4, 6, 8

D 12, 24, 36, 48, 60

The correct answer is C. Find the numbers that multiply to get a product of 12: 1 × 12, 2 × 6, and 3 × 4. Arranged in order, the factors are 1, 2, 3, 4, 6, 12. Look for the list that includes all these factors. Remember that 1 and the number itself are *always* factors of the number. Only choice C includes 1 and 12 as well as the other factors.

1 What are the factors of 16?

A 1, 2, 3, 4, 8   **C** 1, 2, 4, 8, 16

B 1, 2, 8, 16   **D** 2, 4, 6, 8, 16

2 Which is a factor pair for 32?

A 3 and 6   **C** 6 and 8

B 4 and 8   **D** 9 and 4

3 Which shows all the multiples of 5 from 5 to 30?

A 1, 3, 5, 15

B 1, 5, 10, 15, 20

C 5, 10, 20, 30

D 5, 10, 15, 20, 25, 30

4 Which is the least whole number that has factors of 1, 2, 4, 5, 10, and 20?

A 20   **C** 40

B 30   **D** 45

5 Which number is **not** a multiple of 6?

A 36   **C** 54

B 46   **D** 72

6 Which number is a multiple of 3?

A 23   **C** 99

B 49   **D** 100

7 What number has the factor pairs of 2 × 9 and 3 × 6?

A 9   **C** 18

B 12   **D** 24

8 Which number is a multiple of 1, 2, 4, 7, 8, 14, 28, and 56?

A 56   **C** 86

B 76   **D** 122

SAMPLE The numbers 2 and 5 are both factors of 20. Are they a factor pair of 20? Explain.

Answer _____

> ✓ You can check if two numbers are a factor pair by multiplying to find their product: 2 × 5 = 10. So, 2 and 5 are not a factor pair for 20. They are parts of different factor pairs of 20: 2 and 10, and 4 and 5.

9 Ethan says 2, 3, 5, 6, 10, and 15 are all the factors of 30. Is he correct? Explain.

Answer _____

10 Name all the factor pairs for 28.

Answer _____

11 Explain how to find the multiples of 8.

_____

_____

12 The number 40 is a multiple of 4. It is also a multiple of 5. Explain how 40 can be a multiple of two different numbers.

_____

_____

13 The astronomy club meets once every three weeks for a year beginning with the 3rd week. On which weeks of the year will the club meet?

Answer _____

14 Cydney has 36 petunias to plant in equal rows.

Part A Find how many equal rows of petunias Cydney can make. How many petunias will be in each row? Name all the possible ways.

_____

_____

_____

Part B Cydney also has 64 marigolds. She wants to plant them in rows with the same number of flowers as the number of petunias in a row. She plants more than one flower in a row. How many flowers in a row should she plant? How many rows of marigolds would that number make? Explain how you know.

What factors of 64 are also factors of 36?

_____

_____

_____

15 Mr. Groff's class has more than 20 students but fewer than 30. The class was split into 5 equal groups.

Part A How many students are in the class?

Answer _____

Part B Explain how you found your answer.

_____

_____

_____

Prime and Composite Numbers

4.OA.4

A prime number has only one factor pair.

A composite number has more than one factor pair.

The numbers 0 and 1 are *not* prime or composite because they do not have at least two factors.

Even numbers can be divided by 2, so all even numbers have 2 as a factor. All even numbers greater than 2 are composite numbers.

A **prime number** is a whole number that has only two factors, 1 and itself.

7 is a prime number. It has only two factors, 1 and 7.

A whole number that has more than two factors is a **composite number.**

8 is a composite number. Its factors are 1, 2, 4, and 8.

You can decide if a number is prime or composite by finding its factor pairs.

What are the prime numbers less than 10?

Find the factor pairs of each whole number less than 10. You can make a table. Start with 2, because 0 and 1 are not prime or composite numbers.

Whole number	2	3	4	5	6	7	8	9
Factor pairs	1, 2	1, 3	1, 4 2, 2	1, 5	1, 6 2, 3	1, 7	1, 8 2, 4	1, 9 3, 3

Numbers that have only one factor pair are prime, so look for numbers with just one pair: 2, 3, 5, 7

Numbers with more than one factor pair are composite, so look for numbers with more than one pair: 4, 6, 8, 9

SAMPLE Which group shows only the prime numbers between 1 and 12?

    A   1, 2, 3, 5, 11   **C**   2, 3, 5, 7, 9, 11

    B   2, 3, 5, 7, 11   **D**   2, 3, 4, 5, 7, 11

The correct answer is B. Find the numbers between 1 and 12 that have only two factors: 2, 3, 5, 7, and 11. Then look for the answer with those numbers. Choice A is incorrect because 1 has only 1 factor, so it is not prime. Choice C is incorrect because 9 is a composite number. Choice D includes 4, which is composite, so it is incorrect.

1 What are all the prime numbers between 14 and 40?

    A   13, 17, 19, 23, 29, 31

    B   15, 17, 19, 23, 29, 31

    C   17, 19, 23, 29, 31, 37

    D   19, 23, 29, 31, 37, 41

2 Which group shows all the composite numbers between 11 and 20?

    A   12, 14, 15, 16, 18

    B   12, 13, 14, 15, 16, 18

    C   12, 14, 15, 16, 18, 19

    D   12, 14, 16, 18, 20

3 Which statement about 51 is true?

    A   It is prime because it is odd.

    B   It is prime because its factors are 1 and 51.

    C   It is composite because it can be divided by 3.

    D   It is composite because it is even.

4 Which number is a prime number?

    A   54   **C**   77

    B   67   **D**   81

5 Which number is a composite number?

    A   47   **C**   87

    B   71   **D**   89

6 Which type of whole number can be represented by 2 groups of 3?

    A   factor   **C**   composite

    B   prime   **D**   fraction

7 How many factors does a composite number have?

    A   more than two

    B   three—0, 1, and itself

    C   only two

    D   only one

SAMPLE Warren has 23 folding chairs to set up for a meeting. Can he set up the chairs in rows of equal numbers of chairs? Explain.

Answer _____

> Warren can make equal rows only if 23 is a composite number. That is, he can do it if 23 can be divided into equal groups. Find the factor pairs of 23. There is only one pair: 1 and 23. That means 23 is a prime number. Warren cannot set up the chairs in equal rows.

8 Is 21 a prime number or a composite number? Explain how you know.

Answer _____

9 Is the number 49 prime or composite? Explain how you know.

Answer _____

10 Which numbers between 25 and 35 are prime? Which are composite?

Prime _____   Composite _____

11 Luz knows that 95 is a multiple of 5. How does this fact help her decide if 95 is prime or composite?

_____

_____

12 There are 54 oranges in a crate. Harry wants to put them in smaller baskets with the same number of oranges in each. How does knowing if 54 is prime or composite help Harry make the baskets?

_____

_____

_____

13 This chart shows whole numbers from 1 to 100.

X	2	3	4	5	6	7	8	9	10
11	12	13	14	15	16	17	18	19	20
21	22	23	24	25	26	27	28	29	30
31	32	33	34	35	36	37	38	39	40
41	42	43	44	45	46	47	48	49	50
51	52	53	54	55	56	57	58	59	60
61	62	63	64	65	66	67	68	69	70
71	72	73	74	75	76	77	78	79	80
81	82	83	84	85	86	87	88	89	90
91	92	93	94	95	96	97	98	99	100

Part A Explain how to find which numbers on the chart are prime and which are composite.

_____

_____

_____

Part B Use the chart to find all the prime numbers between 1 and 100. Cross out each number that is a multiple of any number other than itself. Then circle each number that has only two factors. List the prime numbers.

All multiples of prime numbers are composite numbers. So find the multiples of 2, of 3, of 5, and so on.

_____

_____

_____

REVIEW

Number Sense

Read each problem. Circle the letter of the best answer.

1 In which number does the 7 have the greatest value?

A   17,042

C   40,172

B   24,701

D   72,401

2 Which shows $(2 \times 10,000) + (6 \times 100) + (8 \times 10) + (5 \times 1)$ in standard form?

A   26,805

C   20,685

B   26,085

D   2,685

3 The number of play tickets sold for Friday, Saturday, and Sunday are 533, 571, and 550. Which list shows these numbers in order from least to greatest?

A   550, 533, 571

C   571, 550, 533

B   533, 550, 571

D   571, 533, 550

4 Which inequality is true?

A $75,205 < 71,204$

B $77,210 < 77,190$

C $81,249 > 81,250$

D $84,005 > 83,989$

5 A farmer harvested 174,521 pounds of potatoes. What is this number rounded to the thousands place?

A   174,000

C   180,000

B   175,000

D   200,000

6 Which shows all the factors of 18?

A   1, 2, 3, 4, 6

C   2, 4, 6, 8, 16, 18

B   1, 2, 4, 6, 18

D   1, 2, 3, 6, 9, 18

7 Which number is a multiple of 4?

A   96

C   98

B   97

D   99

8 Which number is a prime number?

A   9

C   33

B   17

D   51

9 Which number is composite?

A   19

C   49

B   29

D   79

10 Is 29,039 greater than or less than 29,227? Explain how you know.

_____

_____

_____

11 Theodora orders these numbers from greatest to least this way:

80,053, 80,530, 80,350

What mistake did Theodora make?

_____

_____

12 The stamp club collected 1,355 stamps to put on display. Round the number to the nearest hundred.

Answer _____

13 There are 15,705 fish in a school of fish living in a coral reef. Write this number in expanded form.

Answer _____

14 What are the factor pairs for 24?

Answer _____

15 Give an example of a prime number less than 100. Explain what makes your number prime.

_____

_____

16 There are 64 members in the middle school marching band. They will line up in equal rows for a parade.

Part A How many rows could the band members line up in? How many members would be in each row? Name all the ways.

_____

_____

_____

Part B The number of brass players in the marching band is a multiple of 3 that is more than 15 and less than 25. How many brass players could there be? Explain how you found your answer.

_____

_____

_____

17 Jacklyn and James are running in a race. Jacklyn is wearing the number 23. James is wearing the number 39.

Part A Is Jacklyn's number a prime number or a composite number? Explain how you know.

_____

_____

Part B Is James's number a prime number or a composite number? Explain how you know.

_____

_____

Operations

● **Lesson 1 Adding Whole Numbers** reviews how to add two or more multi-digit whole numbers to find the sum.

● **Lesson 2 Subtracting Whole Numbers** reviews how to subtract multi-digit whole numbers to find the difference.

● **Lesson 3 Multiplying Whole Numbers** reviews how to use a model or vertical multiplication to find the product of two whole numbers.

● **Lesson 4 Dividing Whole Numbers** reviews how to use place-value blocks or vertical division to find the quotient of two whole numbers.

Adding Whole Numbers

4.NBT.4

Vertical means "arranged up and down."

The numbers you add are called **addends**. The result is called the **sum**.

The **commutative property** is true for addition. You can change the order of the addends, and the sum stays the same.

$$1 + 4 = 5$$
$$4 + 1 = 5$$

The **associative property** is true for addition. You can group addends in any way, and the sum stays the same.

$$(1 + 4) + 5 = 5 + 5 = 10$$
$$1 + (4 + 5) = 1 + 9 = 10$$
$$(1 + 5) + 4 = 6 + 4 = 10$$

To add multi-digit whole numbers, use a vertical format.

What is the sum of 624 and 793?

First, estimate the sum: $600 + 800 = 1,400$

Next, write the addends in a column. **Align,** or line up, the digits in the same places.

$$\begin{array}{r} 624 \\ +793 \\ \hline \end{array}$$

Add the digits in each column, starting on the right. Add the ones: 4 ones + 3 ones = 7 ones

$$\begin{array}{r} 624 \\ +793 \\ \hline 7 \end{array}$$

Add the tens: 2 tens + 9 tens = 11 tens. When the sum is 10 or more, regroup: 11 tens = 1 hundred 1 ten. Write the 1 ten in the sum. Write the 1 hundred above the hundreds column.

$$\begin{array}{r} {}^{1} \\ 624 \\ +793 \\ \hline 17 \end{array}$$

Add the hundreds: 1 hundred + 6 hundreds + 7 hundreds = 14 hundreds. Regroup: 14 hundreds = 1 thousand 4 hundreds. Write the hundreds in the sum. Write the 1 thousand above the thousands column.

$$\begin{array}{r} {}^{1} \\ 624 \\ +793 \\ \hline 417 \end{array}$$

Add the thousands: $1 + 0 + 0 = 1$. Write the thousands digit in the sum.

$$\begin{array}{r} {}^{1\,1} \\ 624 \\ +793 \\ \hline 1,417 \end{array}$$

Compare your answer to your estimated sum: 1,417 is close to 1,400, so the answer is reasonable.

You can use the same process to find the sum of three or more numbers.

Find the sum of $381 + 93 + 890$.

Write all of the addends in a column. Be sure to correctly align units. Start on the right. Add each column. Regroup as necessary.

The sum is 1,364.

$$\begin{array}{r} {}^{1\,2} \\ 381 \\ 93 \\ +\ 890 \\ \hline 1,364 \end{array}$$

SAMPLE What is the sum of 7,895 + 146?

     A 7,041   **B** 7,941   **C** 8,041   **D** 9,355

> The correct answer is C. One addend has four places and the other has three places. Write the numbers vertically, but be careful to align the numbers on the right, so the ones will be added to ones, the tens to tens, and so on. Then add each column of digits. Regroup as necessary.
>
> ```
>   1 1 1
>   7,895
> +   146
> -------
>   8,041
> ```

1 Add 126 + 573.

  A 689   **C** 789

  B 699   **D** 799

2
```
  1,492
+ 3,156
```

  A 3,648   **C** 4,648

  B 4,548   **D** 4,658

3 Find the sum of 4,707 + 865.

  A 4,562   **C** 5,562

  B 4,572   **D** 5,572

4 What is 367 + 1,654?

  A 1,021   **C** 2,011

  B 1,921   **D** 2,021

5
```
  16,524
+ 31,748
```

  A 47,262   **C** 48,272

  B 48,262   **D** 49,272

6 Solve:

      6,874 + 10,197 = ☐

  A 16,071   **C** 17,061

  B 16,961   **D** 17,071

7 What is the sum of 125 + 362 + 312?

  A 789   **C** 800

  B 799   **D** 809

8 What is 3,994 + 875 + 2,406?

  A 6,275   **C** 7,265

  B 7,176   **D** 7,275

9
```
   5,138
     206
  17,245
+  1,413
```

  A 23,902   **C** 24,002

  B 23,992   **D** 24,003

SAMPLE Sheila added 2,638 and 794 for a sum of 3,322. Sam added the same numbers and got 3,432. Who is wrong and what mistake did that person make?

Answer _____

Set up the numbers vertically and add the digits in the same places, starting on the right. Whenever the sum of a column is 10 or more, regroup. Remember to add the regrouped number in that column. Sheila forgot to add the regrouped numbers.

```
  1 11
  2,638
+   794
  3,432
```

10 Add 429 + 583. Show your work.

Answer _____

11 What is the missing digit in this problem?

Explain how you know.

```
   6,735
+  3,3□8
  10,133
```

_____

_____

12 Abel added 3,286 + 891 and got 12,196. What mistake did he make?

_____

_____

13 Find the sum of 8,039 + 657 + 23,462. Show your work.

Answer _____

14 Explain when and how to regroup in addition.

_____

_____

_____

34 **UNIT 2** ▨▨▨▨▨▨▨▨▨▨▨▨▨▨▨▨▨▨▨▨▨▨▨▨▨▨▨▨
Operations

15 Devora added 1,213 + 89 + 692 and got a sum of 1,984.

Part A Is Devora's answer reasonable? Use estimation to explain
why it is or is not.

_____

_____

_____

Part B Is Devora's answer correct? Find the sum and show
your work.

Answer _____

16 Jason added 728 + 681 + 4,632. His work and the sum he found are
shown below.

$$
\begin{array}{r}
\overset{1}{}\ \overset{1}{}\ \ \\
728 \\
681 \\
+4,632 \\
\hline
5,941
\end{array}
$$

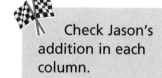

Check Jason's
addition in each
column.

Part A What mistake did Jason make?

_____

_____

Part B Find the correct sum. Show your work.

Answer _____

Subtracting Whole Numbers

4.NBT.4

The result of a subtraction problem is called the **difference.**

Unlike addition, subtraction is *not* commutative. You cannot change the order of the numbers without changing the result.

$$12 - 3 = 9$$
$$3 - 12 \neq 9$$

Regrouping in subtraction is sometimes called "borrowing."

Addition and subtraction are **inverse operations.** You can use addition to check your subtraction.

$$10 - 6 = 4$$
because
$$4 + 6 = 10$$

To subtract whole numbers, use a vertical format.

What is $649 - 263$?

First, estimate the difference: $650 - 260 = 390$

Next, write the number you are subtracting below the number you are subtracting from. Be careful to correctly align digits in the same places.

$$\begin{array}{r} 649 \\ -263 \\ \hline \end{array}$$

Subtract each column, starting on the right.
Subtract the ones: 9 ones − 3 ones = 6 ones

$$\begin{array}{r} 649 \\ -263 \\ \hline 6 \end{array}$$

Subtract the tens. Since 4 tens < 6 tens, you must regroup. Regroup 6 hundreds as 5 hundreds 10 tens. Add the 10 tens to the 4 tens to make 14 tens. Then subtract: 14 tens − 6 tens = 8 tens

$$\begin{array}{r} {}^{5\ 14}\!\!\not{6}\not{4}9 \\ -263 \\ \hline 86 \end{array}$$

Subtract the hundreds: 5 hundreds − 2 hundreds = 3 hundreds

$$\begin{array}{r} {}^{5\ 14}\!\!\not{6}\not{4}9 \\ -263 \\ \hline 386 \end{array}$$

Compare your answer to your estimated difference: 386 is close to 390, so the answer is reasonable.

You can use the same process to subtract across zeros.

Find the difference of $700 - 532$.

The only way to "borrow" 10 from the tens digit in 700 is to first "borrow" 100 from the hundreds digit. Regroup 7 hundreds as 6 hundreds 10 tens. Regroup the 10 tens as 9 tens 10 ones.

First subtract ones.	Subtract tens.	Subtract hundreds.
$\begin{array}{r} {}^{9}\\ {}^{6\ \not{10}\ 10}\\ \not{7}\not{0}\not{0} \\ -532 \\ \hline 8 \end{array}$	$\begin{array}{r} {}^{9}\\ {}^{6\ \not{10}\ 10}\\ \not{7}\not{0}\not{0} \\ -532 \\ \hline 68 \end{array}$	$\begin{array}{r} {}^{9}\\ {}^{6\ \not{10}\ 10}\\ \not{7}\not{0}\not{0} \\ -532 \\ \hline 168 \end{array}$

You can use addition to check your answer: $532 + 168 = 700$

SAMPLE What is 5,807 − 3,634?

A 1,173   B 2,173   C 2,263   D 2,273

The correct answer is B. To find the difference, write
the number being subtracted below the number you are
subtracting from, aligning digits in the same places.
Starting on the right, subtract in each column. Regroup
as necessary.

$$\begin{array}{r} 7\;10 \\ 5,\cancel{8}\cancel{0}7 \\ -3,634 \\ \hline 2,173 \end{array}$$

1 Subtract 496 − 183.

A 213   C 313

B 223   D 323

2   3,369
                −2,274

A 1,025   C 1,095

B 1,085   D 1,195

3 Find the difference.

6,748 − 865 = ☐

A 4,883   C 5,933

B 5,883   D 5,983

4 Solve: 2,573
                −1,648

A 925   C 935

B 926   D 1,935

5 What is 504 − 396?

A 108   C 208

B 118   D 218

6 Subtract:

6,805 − 797 = ☐

A 5,008   C 6,008

B 5,108   D 6,118

7   3,007
                −1,488

A 1,519   C 1,619

B 1,529   D 2,619

8 Find the difference.

8,200
−5,639

A 2,561   C 2,661

B 2,571   D 3,661

SAMPLE To subtract 8,258 − 762, which places do you need to regroup? Explain.

Answer _____

✓ If the digit you are subtracting is larger than the digit you are subtracting from, you need to regroup the next place to the left. In the tens place, 6 is greater than 5. So you need to regroup the hundreds as 1 hundred 10 tens, so you will have 15 tens. In the hundreds, 7 is greater than 1 hundred. So you will also need to regroup the thousands as 7 thousands 10 hundreds to make 11 hundreds.

9 Subtract 509 − 423. Show your work.

Answer _____

10 What is the missing digit in this problem? Explain how you know.

$$\begin{array}{r} 3{,}048 \\ -\ 1{,}\square25 \\ \hline 1{,}423 \end{array}$$

_____

_____

11 Subtract 716 from 6,438. Show your work.

Answer _____

12 Find the difference of 8,024 − 979. Show your work.

Answer _____

13 How can you check your answer to problem 12?

_____

_____

14 Alan subtracted 3,318 − 1,506 and found the difference to be 2,812.

Part A Is Alan's answer reasonable? Explain why or why not.

_____

_____

Part B Find the difference. Show your work.

Answer _____

15 Meena subtracted 2,002 − 1,683. Her work and the difference she found are shown below.

$$
\begin{array}{r}
{}^{9}\\
{}_{1\ 10\ 10\ 12}\\
\cancel{2{,}00\!\!\!/2}\\
-\,1{,}683\\
\hline
419
\end{array}
$$

Part A What mistake did Meena make?

_____

_____

_____

_____

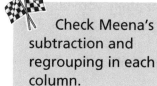

Check Meena's subtraction and regrouping in each column.

Part B Find the correct difference. Show your work.

Answer _____

Multiplying Whole Numbers

4.NBT.5

An **array** is a model using rows and columns. When they are connected, the array is an **area model.**

The **commutative property** is true for multiplication. Changing the order of the numbers does not change the product.

$3 \times 14 = 42$
is the same as
$14 \times 3 = 42$

In multiplication the numbers you multiply are called **factors.** The result is called the **product.**

A model can help you picture multiplication.

Use an array to model 3×14.

Remember that 14 is the same as $10 + 4$. So 3×14 is the same as multiplying $3 \times (10 + 4)$. Draw a model like this:

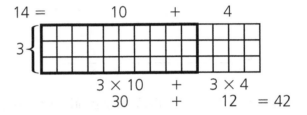

Multiply the tens: $3 \times 10 = 30$

Multiply the ones: $3 \times 4 = 12$

Add the products: $30 + 12 = 42$

A faster way to multiply is with vertical multiplication.

Multiply 18×32.

First, estimate the product: $20 \times 30 = 600$

Next, multiply by the ones. Regroup where you need to.
$8 \times 32 = (8 \times 30) + (8 \times 2) = 240 + 16 = 256$

$$\begin{array}{r} 1 \\ 32 \\ \times 18 \\ \hline 256 \end{array}$$

Write a placeholder 0 in the ones place of the next partial product.
Then, multiply by the tens digit: $10 \times 32 = 320$

$$\begin{array}{r} 32 \\ \times 18 \\ \hline 256 \\ 320 \end{array}$$

Finally, add the partial products: $256 + 320 = 576$
The product of 18×32 is 576.

$$\begin{array}{r} 32 \\ \times 18 \\ \hline 256 \\ 320 \\ \hline 576 \end{array}$$

This product is close to the estimate, so it is reasonable.

SAMPLE Multiply 6 × 3,427.

A 18,562   B 20,522   C 20,462   D 20,562

The correct answer is D. To find the product, write one factor below the other, aligning the same places. Starting on the right, multiply the bottom factor times each digit in the top factor. Regroup as necessary. Remember to add the regrouped number at the top *after* multiplying that place.

$$\begin{array}{r} {\scriptstyle 2\ 14} \\ 3{,}427 \\ \times 6 \\ \hline 20{,}562 \end{array}$$

1 Multiply: 372
                      ×3

A 916   C 1,046

B 1,016   D 1,116

2   564
                  ×4

A 2,056   C 2,256

B 2,246   D 2,264

3 Find the product.

8 × 709 = ☐

A 5,602   C 5,752

B 5,672   D 6,372

4 Solve: 458
                   ×7

A 2,806   C 3,206

B 3,156   D 3,213

5 What is the product of 4 × 1,261?

A 4,044   C 5,044

B 4,844   D 5,084

6 Multiply: 3,785
                      ×6

A 18,680   C 22,710

B 22,210   D 22,810

7 Solve 9 × 6,243.

A 54,187   C 56,167

B 54,887   D 56,187

8 Find the product.

7,987
×8

A 56,896   C 63,846

B 63,296   D 63,896

SAMPLE Find 76 × 52.

Answer _____

> To find the product, write one factor below the other factor. Starting on the right, multiply each digit of the bottom factor times the top factor. Regroup as needed. Multiply by the ones: 6 × 52 = 312. Then multiply by the tens: 70 × 52 = 3,640. Add the partial products: 312 + 3,640 = 3,952. The product is 3,952.

$$\begin{array}{r} 52 \\ \times 76 \\ \hline 312 \\ +3{,}640 \\ \hline 3{,}952 \end{array}$$

9 Multiply 13 × 32. Show your work.

Answer _____

10 Find 63 × 58. Show your work.

Answer _____

11 Without multiplying, tell which has the greater product: 3 × 495 or 4 × 387? Explain how you know.

_____

_____

12 Explain when and how you regroup in multiplication.

_____

_____

_____

_____

13 Sophie multiplied 7 × 5,898 and found the product to be 41,186.

Part A Is Sophie's answer reasonable? Explain why it is or is not.

_____

_____

_____

> What does 5,898 round to? What is the estimated product?

Part B Find the product. Show your work.

Answer _____

14 Thomas multiplied 52 × 48. His work and the product he found are shown below.

$$
\begin{array}{r}
48 \\
\times 52 \\
\hline
96 \\
240 \\
\hline
336
\end{array}
$$

Part A What mistake did Thomas make?

_____

_____

_____

Part B Find the correct product. Show your work.

Answer _____

Dividing Whole Numbers

4.NBT.6

The **dividend** is the number being divided. The **divisor** is the number doing the dividing. The **quotient** is the result.

Estimate the quotient first to know where to start the quotient.

A compatible number for 492 is 480, and 480 ÷ 8 is 60. So the quotient should start in the tens place.

Divide from left to right. If the digit in a place is not large enough to divide, regroup and divide the next place to the right.

Multiplication and division are **inverse operations.** Use multiplication to check division.

8 × 62 = 496

Place-value blocks can help you picture division.

What is 32 ÷ 2?

Divide the tens.   Regroup 1 ten as 10 ones.
                        Divide the ones.

3 tens ÷ 2 = 1 ten   12 ones ÷ 2 = 6 ones

So 32 ÷ 2 = 1 ten + 6 ones = 16.

A faster way to divide is with vertical division.

What is the quotient of 496 ÷ 8?

4 hundreds cannot be divided by 8. So, move one place to the right and divide the tens: 49 tens ÷ 8 = 6

$$\begin{array}{r} 6 \\ 8\overline{)496} \end{array}$$

Multiply: 6 × 8 = 48
Then subtract: 49 − 48 = 1
That is 1 ten to be regrouped as ones.

$$\begin{array}{r} 6 \\ 8\overline{)496} \\ -48 \\ \hline 1 \end{array}$$

Bring down the 6 from the dividend.
Then divide the ones: 16 ÷ 8 = 2

$$\begin{array}{r} 6 \\ 8\overline{)496} \\ -48\downarrow \\ \hline 16 \end{array}$$

Multiply: 2 × 8 = 16
Then subtract: 16 − 16 = 0

So the quotient of 496 ÷ 8 is 62.

$$\begin{array}{r} 62 \\ 8\overline{)496} \\ -48 \\ \hline 16 \\ -16 \\ \hline 0 \end{array}$$

SAMPLE Divide: 4)968

    A 192   **B** 240   **C** 242   **D** 247

The correct answer is C. To find the quotient, divide the dividend from left to right by the divisor. Divide the hundreds, multiply, and subtract. Regroup and divide the tens. Multiply and subtract. Then divide the ones.

```
  242
4)968
 -8
  16
 -16
  08
  -8
   0
```

1   3)72

  A 14   **C** 24

  B 23   **D** 26

2 Find 92 ÷ 4.

  A 16   **C** 26

  B 23   **D** 28

3 Solve: 7)98

  A 12   **C** 14

  B 13   **D** 16

4 Divide 369 ÷ 3.

  A 123   **C** 133

  B 132   **D** 142

5 Divide: 5)355

  A 70   **C** 701

  B 71   **D** 710

6 Find the quotient.

     594 ÷ 9 = ☐

  A 64   **C** 67

  B 66   **D** 76

7   2)6,284

  A 2,957   **C** 3,042

  B 3,032   **D** 3,142

8 What is 6,712 ÷ 8?

  A 751   **C** 842

  B 839   **D** 1,139

SAMPLE Find the quotient of 5,154 ÷ 6.

Answer _____

Set up the problem vertically, and find the first place
you can divide by 6. You cannot divide 5 thousands
by 6, so look at dividing 51 hundreds by 6: 51 ÷ 6 = 8.
Multiply and subtract. Bring down the digit in the next
place and divide. Repeat the division until you have a
remainder of 0.

$$
\begin{array}{r}
859 \\
6\overline{)5,154} \\
-48 \\
\hline
35 \\
-30 \\
\hline
54 \\
-54 \\
\hline
0
\end{array}
$$

9 Solve 301 ÷ 7. Show your work.

Answer _____

10 Find 1,568 ÷ 8. Show your work.

Answer _____

11 What is 5,127 ÷ 3? Show your work.

Answer _____

12 Without finding the quotients, tell which has the greater quotient:
2,686 ÷ 3 or 5,610 ÷ 7? Explain.

_____

_____

13 Why does the quotient 36 ÷ 3 have two digits, but the quotient
36 ÷ 6 has only one digit? Explain.

_____

_____

_____

14 Alma divided 3,512 ÷ 8. Her work and the quotient she found are shown below.

$$
\begin{array}{r}
440 \\
8\overline{)3{,}512} \\
-3\,2 \\
\hline
31 \\
-28 \\
\hline
32 \\
-32 \\
\hline
0
\end{array}
$$

Check Alma's division, multiplication, and subtraction for each number in the quotient.

Part A What mistake did Alma make?

_____

_____

_____

Part B Find the correct quotient. Show your work.

Answer _____

REVIEW

Operations

Read each problem. Circle the letter of the best answer.

1 Find the sum of 224 + 573.

- **A** 697
- **B** 778
- **C** 787
- **D** 797

2 Subtract:
$$\begin{array}{r} 7,965 \\ -3,274 \end{array}$$

- **A** 4,671
- **B** 4,691
- **C** 4,781
- **D** 4,791

3 Find the product of 7 × 618.

- **A** 4,226
- **B** 4,276
- **C** 4,316
- **D** 4,326

4 $3\overline{)936}$

- **A** 231
- **B** 302
- **C** 312
- **D** 313

5 Add:
$$\begin{array}{r} 25,734 \\ +14,328 \end{array}$$

- **A** 30,062
- **B** 39,062
- **C** 40,052
- **D** 40,062

6
$$\begin{array}{r} 4,036 \\ -845 \end{array}$$

- **A** 3,191
- **B** 3,201
- **C** 3,291
- **D** 4,191

7 Multiply:
$$\begin{array}{r} 5,264 \\ \times9 \end{array}$$

- **A** 45,376
- **B** 47,176
- **C** 47,316
- **D** 47,376

8 Solve: $8\overline{)584}$

- **A** 63
- **B** 73
- **C** 74
- **D** 83

9
$$\begin{array}{r} 96 \\ \times87 \end{array}$$

- **A** 1,430
- **B** 7,952
- **C** 8,312
- **D** 8,352

10 Divide 5,488 by 7.

- **A** 641
- **B** 779
- **C** 784
- **D** 844

11 Subtract 7,300 − 4,326. Show your work.

Answer _____

12 Find the product of 76 × 94. Show your work.

Answer _____

13 Divide 3,933 ÷ 9. Show your work.

Answer _____

14 How can you use multiplication to check your answer in problem 13?

_____

_____

15 Explain why the quotient 480 ÷ 4 includes three digits, but the quotient 480 ÷ 6 includes only two digits.

_____

_____

_____

16 Look at this problem.

$$17,596 + 453 + 1,034 = \square$$

Part A Find the sum. Show your work.

Answer _____

Part B Explain how you can use inverse operations to check your answer to part A.

_____

_____

_____

17 Josie multiplied 58×96. Her work and the product she found are shown below.

$$
\begin{array}{r}
96 \\
\times 58 \\
\hline
768 \\
480 \\
\hline
1,248
\end{array}
$$

Part A What mistake did Josie make?

_____

_____

_____

Part B Find the correct product. Show your work.

Answer _____

Solving Problems

● **Lesson 1 Representing Word Problems** reviews how to represent a word problem using an expression or an equation.

● **Lesson 2 Solving One-Step Word Problems** reviews how to solve one-step word problems using multiplication or division.

● **Lesson 3 Solving Two-Step Word Problems** reviews how to solve two-step word problems using the four operations.

● **Lesson 4 Estimation** reviews how to use estimation to check if an answer to a problem is reasonable.

Representing Word Problems

4.OA.3

Key words are clues to operations.

Addition (+)
 add
 sum
 more than
 in all
 total
 combined

Subtraction (−)
 subtract
 difference
 less
 fewer than
 minus

Multiplication (×)
 multiply
 product
 times
 groups of

Divide (÷)
 divide
 quotient
 equal groups
 share
 split equally

A symbol or letter that stands for a number in an expression or number sentence is called a *variable.*

To solve a word problem, you first need to translate the words in it to expressions. An **expression** is a grouping of numbers and operations that show the value of something.

Flora has 2 apples. Darryl has 3 more apples than Flora. Write an expression that shows how many apples Darryl has.

The problem tells you how many apples Flora has: 2

It tells you how many apples Darryl has **in terms of** the number of apples Flora has: 3 more than Flora

The word *more* tells you to add: + 3

Combine the numbers and operation sign to represent the number of apples Darryl has: 2 + 3

To solve a word problem, write an equation. An **equation** is a number sentence that says two expressions are equal.

Some friends were having a picnic in the park. Later, 4 people went home. There were 5 people left at the picnic. How many people were at the picnic at the beginning?

Think about what you know.
• the number of people who went home: 4
• the number of people left after 4 went home: 5

Think about what you are being asked to find.
• the number of people at the picnic before anyone left: ?
This number is unknown, so use a letter to represent it: n

The phrase *4 people went home* tells you to subtract 4 people from the number at the start of the picnic: $n - 4$

This expression $n - 4$ is equal to 5, the number left. Write an equation using these two expressions: $n - 4 = 5$

This equation says that the number of people at the picnic, less the number who went home, is equal to the number left.

SAMPLE Gino is packing 24 books in boxes. He puts 6 books in each box. Which equation shows how many boxes Gino uses?

A $6 + n = 24$

B $n \div 6 = 24$

C $24 - n = 6$

D $6 \times n = 24$

The correct answer is D. To find how many groups of 6 can be made from 24, you can use multiplication or division. If n represents the number of boxes, then multiplying n by 6 books will equal 24: $6 \times n = 24$. This can also be shown using division: $24 \div n = 6$. Choice B uses division, but it does not show the numbers and variable in the correct positions. So it is incorrect.

1 Ji Sun had 20 stickers. She gave 6 stickers to a friend. Then Ji Sun's sister gave her 8 more stickers. Which expression shows how many stickers Ji Sun now has?

A $20 - 6 + 8$

B $6 + 8 - 20$

C $20 + 6 - 8$

D $8 - 6 + 20$

2 Benny takes care of 25 goats. He puts 5 goats in each pen. Which expression shows how many pens Benny uses?

A 25×5

B $25 \div 5$

C $25 - 5$

D $25 + 5$

3 Some students are visiting a science museum. There are 3 buses and 27 students are on each bus. Which expression shows the total number of students visiting the museum?

A $27 \div 3$

B 27×3

C $27 - 3$

D $27 + 3$

4 Toni had $45 in a savings account. She took out some money and then had $34 in the account. Which equation shows this?

A $45 \times d = 34$

B $45 \div d = 34$

C $45 + d = 34$

D $45 - d = 34$

5 Becca buys 2 pounds of red plums and 3 pounds of black plums. The plums cost $2 per pound. Which expression shows how much Becca pays for all the plums?

A $(2 + 3) \times 2$

B $(2 + 3) - 2$

C $(2 \times 3) - 2$

D $(2 + 3) \div 2$

6 A spider lays some eggs, but 1,250 eggs do not hatch. Only 1,750 eggs hatch. Which equation could be solved to find how many eggs the spider laid?

A $1,750 - e = 1,250$

B $1,250 - e = 1,750$

C $e - 1,250 = 1,750$

D $1,750 - 1,250 = e$

SAMPLE Allison collects postcards from around the world. She displays them on the wall in 5 rows of 6 postcards each. Write an expression to show the number of postcards that Allison has in her display.

Answer _____

✓ The problem tells you that there are *6 postcards each* in the rows, so the rows are equal groups. Rows of equal numbers make an array, which represents multiplication. To find the total of a number of equal groups, multiply. So the number expression that shows the number of postcards is 5×6.

7 Hiroshi baked c oatmeal cookies for a school bake sale. He sold 16 cookies and had 12 left at the end of the sale. Write a number sentence you could solve to find the number of cookies he made.

Answer _____

8 One day, 7 inches of snow fell. The next day, 3 inches of snow melted. Two days later, it snowed 4 more inches. Write an expression to represent the amount of snow on the ground now.

Answer _____

9 Daniel wrote the number sentence $84 \times r = 12$ to represent the word problem below.

Alec is wrapping 84 dishes in bubble wrap. He uses one roll of wrap for 12 dishes. How many rolls of bubble wrap will Alec use?

Is Daniel's number sentence correct? Explain.

_____

_____

_____

_____

10 Roma Pizza sells pizzas in four sizes.

ROMA PIZZA

Size	Servings	Price
Small	4	$10
Medium	6	$12
Large	8	$14
Extra-Large	10	$16

Part A Use the information in the table to write a word problem for the expression below.

$$\$10 + \$16$$

_____

_____

_____

Part B Arina orders 2 extra-large pizzas for a party. She wants each person to have 2 slices. Arina says the number sentence $2 \times p = 20$ represents the number of people 2 pies will serve. Stavros says $20 \div p = 2$ represents the number of people the pizzas will serve. Who is correct? Explain.

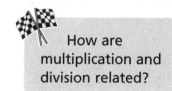

How are multiplication and division related?

_____

_____

_____

_____

_____

Solving One-Step Word Problems

4.OA.1, 4.OA.2

Other word problems that involve comparisons can be solved using addition or subtraction.

Sean's dog is 8 inches taller than Hugo's dog. If Sean's dog is 32 inches tall, how tall is Hugo's dog?

These problems do **not** use words like *times as* or *twice as.*

Multiplication and division are opposite, or **inverse,** operations. This means you can think of $2 \times n = 4$ as $4 \div 2 = n$ and solve the expression.

Many word problems can be solved using multiplication or division. Some of these problems involve comparing amounts or measurements. They may contain phrases like *times as* or *twice as.*

Sean's dog weighs twice as much as Hugo's dog. If Sean's dog weighs 40 pounds, how much does Hugo's dog weigh?

Look for phrases you can use to write an equation.
- Sean's dog weighs *40 pounds.*
- Sean's dog weighs *twice as much* as Hugo's dog.

Write an equation using a letter for the number you do not know, the weight of Hugo's dog.

$$2 \times n = 40$$

Solve your equation for the unknown number. Multiplication and division are opposites, so you can divide 40 by 2 to find *n.*

$2 \times n = 40$ is the same as $40 \div 2 = n = 20$.

Hugo's dog weighs 20 pounds.

Other problems ask *how many in each group* or *how many groups there are.* Multiply or divide to solve these problems, too.

One wall of a building contains 30 windows. There are equal rows of windows with 6 windows in each row. How many rows of windows are there?

Identify the key words and phrases in the problem.
- There are *30 windows.*
- The windows are in *equal rows of 6 windows.*

Write an equation using a letter for the quantity you do not know, the number of rows.

$$6 \times r = 30$$

Solve the equation.

$$6 \times r = 30 \quad \rightarrow \quad 30 \div 6 = r = 5$$

There are 5 rows of windows.

SAMPLE Crystal is 18 years old. She is 3 times older than her cousin, Jack. How old is Jack?

    A 3   **B** 6   **C** 15   **D** 54

> The correct answer is B. If *n* represents Jack's age, then 3 times *n* is equal to Crystal's age: $3 \times n = 18$. To solve this equation, use the opposite operation, division. Divide 18 by 3 to find the value of *n*: $18 \div 3 = 6$. So Jack is 6 years old.

1 The United States has 100 senators who represent the 50 states in the government. Each state has an equal number of senators. How many senators represent each state?

    A 150   **C** 5

    B 10   **D** 2

2 Indira surveyed fourth graders about their favorite sports. Four times as many students chose baseball as chose tennis. If 36 students chose baseball, how many students chose tennis? Use this equation to solve the problem: $4 \times t = 36$.

    A 40   **C** 9

    B 32   **D** 8

3 Sylvie buys 64 tiles. She puts the tiles in 8 equal rows. How many tiles are in each row?

    A 8   **C** 56

    B 12   **D** 72

4 Mrs. Vargas biked 4 miles on Monday. On Tuesday, she biked twice as far. How many miles did she bike on Tuesday?

    A 2   **C** 8

    B 4   **D** 12

5 Nobu is planting 48 lettuce plants. He plants 6 lettuce plants in each row. How many rows does he plant? Use this equation to solve the problem: $6 \times n = 48$.

    A 6   **C** 14

    B 8   **D** 42

6 Jaime finds an unusual bug outside. The bug is 5 times as long as it is wide. The bug is 10 cm long. How wide is it?

    A 15 cm   **C** 5 cm

    B 7 cm   **D** 2 cm

SAMPLE Mr. Vashin has 72 roses that he is using in flower arrangements. He makes 8 identical arrangements. How many roses does Mr. Vashin put in each arrangement?

Answer _____

> The problem tells you that there are 72 roses and 8 arrangements. Each arrangement has an equal number of roses, r. The number sentence $8 \times r = 72$ shows this situation. You can solve the equation for r by dividing: $72 \div 8 = r = 9$. Mr. Vashin puts 9 roses in each arrangement.

7 At a wedding dinner, 88 guests are seated at t tables. If 8 guests are seated at each table, how many tables are there? Draw a picture to help you solve the problem.

Answer _____

8 Lina packs the same number of doughnuts in each box. How many doughnuts does Lina pack in each box?

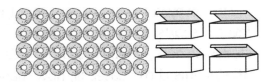

Answer _____

9 Sasha read the following problem.

> Two buses are taking campers to summer camp. Bus A has twice as many students as bus B. Bus A has 48 students. How many students are on bus B?

Sasha wrote the equation $2 \times 48 = n$, where n represents the number of students on bus B. She says there are 96 students on bus B. Is she correct? Explain how you know.

_____

_____

_____

10 The Environment Club will hold a meeting in the room shown below.

30 feet

Part A The dimensions of the room are shown in the diagram. The length is twice the width. How wide is the room? Write and solve an equation that shows this.

Answer _____

Part B Scott is setting up chairs in the room. There are 84 chairs. Scott wants to set up equal rows with 7 chairs in each row. Scott calculates there will be 12 rows. Is he correct? Explain.

You can draw an array to help you decide if Scott's answer is correct.

_____

_____

_____

_____

Solving Two-Step Word Problems

4.OA.1, 4.OA.3

Follow these four steps to solve a word problem.

1. Read the problem carefully.
2. Plan how you will solve it.
3. Solve the problem.
4. Check your answer.

You can write a two-step problem as a single equation:

$$(5 \times 5) + x = 35$$

Addition and subtraction are inverse operations. You can solve an addition equation by subtracting.

Think carefully about what the problem asks. Sometimes you need to round a remainder up. Other times you can ignore a remainder.

Some word problems require two steps to solve.

Rachel earns $5 an hour baby-sitting. Last week she worked for 5 hours. How much more money does Rachel need to buy a watch for $35?

Identify what you know and what you need to know.
- Rachel earns *$5 an hour* and worked *5 hours.*
- *How much more* money does she need to have $35?

Before you can find how much more money Rachel needs, you have to find out how much she earned: $5 × 5 hours = $25

Now you know that Rachel has $25. You know the watch costs $35. Write an equation to show how much more money Rachel needs.

$$25 + x = 35$$

Solve the equation. Use the inverse operation.

$$25 + x = 35 \quad \rightarrow \quad 35 - 25 = 10$$

Rachel needs $10 more.

Sometimes you need to interpret a remainder to solve a problem.

A group of 34 children are at an amusement park. Tickets for the Ferris wheel come in packs of 10 for $12 a pack. How much will it cost for all 34 children to ride the Ferris wheel?

First, divide 34 children by 10 tickets to find out how many packs of tickets they need: 34 ÷ 10 = 3 R4

Interpret the remainder. Since tickets come in packs of 10, 4 packs are needed for everyone to have a ticket. Now multiply to find the total cost.

$$4 \times \$12 = 48$$

It will cost $48 for all 34 children to ride the Ferris wheel.

SAMPLE Raisa has 3 more paper clips than Joe. Paige has twice as many paper clips as Raisa. Paige has 14 paper clips. How many paper clips does Joe have?

A 4   **B** 10   **C** 11   **D** 25

The correct answer is A. Paige has 14 paper clips and this number is twice as many as Raisa has. If r represents the number Raisa has, then $2 \times r = 14$. Since $2 \times 7 = 14$, Raisa has 7 paper clips. Raisa has 3 more than Joe. If j is the number Joe has, then $j + 3 = 7$. Solve: $4 + 3 = 7$, so Joe has 4 paper clips.

1 A group of 12 girls and 8 boys are going canoeing. Each canoe can hold 3 people. How many canoes will they need?

A 4   **C** 7

B 6   **D** 20

2 Dipak buys a 94-page book. The first day, he reads 24 pages. The next day, he reads another 32 pages. How many pages does Dipak have left to read?

A 20   **C** 48

B 38   **D** 56

3 Jake has 36 comic books. His brother has twice as many comic books. How many comic books do they have altogether?

A 62   **C** 102

B 72   **D** 108

4 Pedro is packing 90 flowerpots into boxes. He has 8 boxes that will each hold 9 flowerpots. How many flowerpots will not fit into the boxes?

A 5   **C** 18

B 8   **D** 72

5 Mort buys some T-shirts online. Each T-shirt costs $7. The shipping charge for all of them is $4. If the total comes to $60, how many T-shirts does Mort buy?

A 7   **C** 16

B 8   **D** 56

6 At Sira's school, 96 students signed up for photo classes. There were 23 third graders and 36 fourth graders. The rest were fifth graders. How many fifth graders signed up for the class? Use this equation to help you solve the problem: $23 + 36 + n = 96$.

A 16   **C** 47

B 37   **D** 59

SAMPLE Amy has 3 times as many stickers as Naomi. Naomi has 10 fewer stickers than Rosa. Rosa has 26 stickers. How many stickers does Amy have?

Answer _____

> ✓ Before you can find how many stickers Amy has, you need to know how many stickers Naomi has. Naomi has 10 fewer stickers than Rosa has: 26 − 10 = 16 stickers. Amy has 3 times as many stickers. So Amy has 3 × 16 or 48 stickers.

7 Luisa buys 8 loaves of bread on sale for $3 a loaf. How much change did she get from $40? Show your work.

Answer _____

8 Andrew is making birdhouses. Each birdhouse requires 4 feet of board. If Andrew has 30 feet of wooden boards, can he make 7 birdhouses? Explain.

_____

_____

_____

9 Kim buys 5 packages of batteries. Each package contains 4 batteries. She uses 9 batteries for some remote controls and her digital camera. How many batteries does she have left?

Answer _____

10 Kurt gets $6 a week for doing chores. How many weeks will it take him to save $50 if he already has $10 saved? Explain how you found your answer.

_____

_____

_____

11 Doug owns a popular diner in town. The menu is shown below.

DOUG'S DINER

Salad	$5
Hamburger	$7
Fish Sandwich	$5
Chicken Fingers	$4
French Fries	$2
Bottled Water	$1
Orange Juice	$2
Milk	$1

Part A Earl and his friends order 2 hamburgers and some salads. If they spent $24 in all, how many salads did they buy? Explain the steps you took to solve the problem.

_____

_____

_____

_____

Part B Mia and 7 people from her family are having dinner at the diner. They have $75 to pay for dinner. Do they have enough money for each person to order a hamburger and fries? Explain.

What do you need to know before you can answer the question?

_____

_____

_____

_____

Estimation

4.OA.3

When you break apart a number, you are renaming it as a sum.

14 = 10 + 4

Notice the pattern. The product has the same number of zeros as both factors. A quotient has the number of zeros left after subtracting the number of zeros in the divisor from the number of zeros in the dividend.

To estimate a product or quotient, use **compatible numbers,** numbers that are easy to use.

What is 220 ÷ 7?

Use 210 instead of 220.

210 ÷ 7 = 30

You can use **mental math** to check the reasonableness of addition or subtraction. Here are two strategies.

Diana has $135 in a savings account. She deposits $49. How much money does she have now?

1. You can **break apart** the numbers. Think: $49 = $5 + $44

$$\$135 + \$5 = \$140$$
$$\$140 + \$44 = \$184$$

2. You can use **compensation.** First, make a ten: 49 + 1 = 50

$$\$135 + \$50 = \$185$$

Now subtract 1 from the answer.

$$\$185 - \$1 = \$184$$

You can use mental math for multiplication or division.

A bakery makes 600 muffins a day. How many muffins does the bakery make in 90 days?

You can use **patterns** to multiply or divide.

$$6 \times 9 = 54$$
$$6 \times 90 = 540$$
$$60 \times 90 = 5,400$$
$$600 \times 90 = 54,000 \text{ muffins}$$

You can use **estimation** to check the reasonableness of addition or subtraction. Here are two strategies.

Estimate 4,558 − 2,384.

1. You can use **rounding.**

4,558	→	4,600
−2,384	→	−2,400
		2,200

2. You can use **front-end estimation.**

4,558	→	4,000
−2,384	→	−2,000
		2,000

SAMPLE Preeti is packing CDs in 7 boxes. Each box contains 112 CDs. Using rounding, what is the best estimate of the total number of CDs?

A 120   **B** 770   **C** 840   **D** 1,200

The correct answer is B. To estimate the total number of CDs, round 112 to 110. Then multiply: 7 × 110 = 770. So there are about 770 CDs in all.

1 Ms. Garcia's class raised $517 for a school fundraiser. Mr. Foster's class raised $685. Using front-end estimation, what is the best estimate of the total amount of money raised by both classes?

A $1,000   **C** $1,200

B $1,100   **D** $1,300

2 A theater put on 806 performances during 9 months of the year. What is the best estimate of the average number of performances put on each month?

A 8   **C** 50

B 25   **D** 80

3 One month, Mr. Lim flew 1,236 miles for work. The next month, he flew 1,844 miles. Rounding to the nearest thousand, what is the best estimate of total distance that Mr. Lim flew during the 2 months?

A 900 miles   **C** 2,000 miles

B 1,000 miles   **D** 3,000 miles

4 The Empire State Building in New York is 1,454 feet tall. The Willis Tower in Chicago is 1,730 feet tall. Rounding to the nearest hundred, what is the best estimate of the difference in the buildings' heights?

A 100 feet   **C** 300 feet

B 200 feet   **D** 400 feet

5 A community soup kitchen serves 218 meals each week. What is the best estimate for the number of meals it serves in 12 weeks?

A 20   **C** 2,400

B 240   **D** 4,800

6 At a zoo, a male brown bear has a mass of 648 kg. A female black bear has a mass of 162 kg. Using front-end estimation, what is the best estimate for the difference in the bears' masses?

A 400 kg   **C** 500 kg

B 450 kg   **D** 550 kg

SAMPLE Miguel wants to sort 708 baseball cards into boxes that hold 80 cards each. Use compatible numbers to estimate the number of boxes that Miguel needs for his cards.

Answer _____

A compatible number is one that is close to 708 and can be divided evenly by 80. To make sure that Miguel has enough boxes, choose a number greater than 708. Use 720 instead of 708 because $72 \div 8 = 9$. So $720 \div 80 = 9$. Miguel needs 9 boxes for his cards.

7 Kento used compensation to mentally solve $384 - 57$. He thought this way:

$$384 - 57$$
$$57 + 3 = 60$$
$$384 - 60 = 324$$
$$\text{So } 384 - 57 = 324$$

Is Kento's thinking correct? Explain.

_____

_____

_____

8 The table shows how many pennies Caryn collected in 3 months. Caryn calculated the total was 2,554 pennies. Is Caryn's answer reasonable? Use rounding to check and explain.

Month	Pennies Collected
April	1,115
May	843
June	596

_____

_____

_____

9 The table below shows the number of visitors to a park from April to July.

VISITORS TO COLD CREEK PARK

Month	Number of Visitors
April	2,109
May	1,057
June	2,815
July	3,664

Part A How many more people visited the park in June and July than in April and May? Explain the steps you took to solve the problem.

_____

_____

_____

_____

Part B Use an estimation strategy to check if your answer is reasonable. Explain what you did.

_____

_____

_____

_____

_____

_____

Choose a strategy that will give you an estimate close to the actual answer. In this case, is rounding a better strategy to use than front-end estimation?

REVIEW

Solving Problems

Read each problem. Circle the letter of the best answer.

1 Holly is putting 56 chairs in 8 equal rows. How many chairs are in each row?

A 5   C 22

B 7   D 48

2 Serge drives 42 miles east to a mall. Then he drives 6 miles west to a diner for lunch. He then drives another 23 miles east. Which expression shows how far from home Serge has traveled?

A 42 + 6 + 23   C 42 − 6 + 23

B 42 + 6 − 23   D 42 − 6 − 23

3 There are 12 cases of rings at a jewelry store. There are 168 rings in each case. Using rounding, what is the best estimate for the total number of rings in the cases?

A 1,450   C 1,700

B 1,500   D 2,600

4 There are twice as many bicycles as cars in a parking lot. If there are 34 bicycles, how many cars are in the parking lot?

A 17   C 51

B 29   D 68

5 Shira has 10 pink envelopes. She has 4 fewer white envelopes than pink ones. She has 3 times as many blue envelopes as white ones. How many blue envelopes does Shira have?

A 6   C 30

B 18   D 42

6 Brad has 73 marbles. He gives some marbles to a friend. Now Brad has 48 marbles left. Which equation shows how many marbles he gave his friend?

A $n + 73 = 48$ C $73 − n = 48$

B $73 \div n = 48$ D $48 \times n = 73$

7 Fiona has 43 dolls. Her sister has 49 dolls. They pack all the dolls in boxes of 8. How many boxes do they need?

A 6   C 11

B 7   D 12

8 According to a survey, 4 times as many students prefer swimming as prefer skating. If 64 students prefer swimming, which equation shows how many prefer skating?

A $4 \times n = 64$ C $n \div 4 = 64$

B $4 + n = 64$ D $n − 4 = 64$

9 The average weight of a male giraffe is 2,600 lb. The average weight of a female giraffe is 1,800 lb. Using front-end estimation, what is the difference in average weight?

Answer _____

10 Ward is twice as old as Anita. Anita is 6 years younger than Jess. If Jess is 19, then how old is Ward? Explain.

_____

_____

11 Tyler used patterns to solve the expression 20 × 120. He said that since 2 × 12 = 24, then 20 × 120 = 240. Is he correct? Explain.

_____

_____

12 A toy store makes up *n* grab bags that contain 7 toys in each bag. There are a total of 105 toys in the grab bags. Write an equation that shows this situation.

Answer _____

13 Two classes are having a pizza party. One class has 24 students, and the other class has 38 students. One large pizza serves 8 people. If 7 large pizzas are ordered, will there be enough for each student to get 1 slice? Explain.

_____

_____

_____

_____

14 Cullen is putting candles on tables at a restaurant. There are 19 tables in the restaurant, and each table gets 2 candles. How many candles does Cullen need?

Answer _____

15 A drum-and-bugle corps is performing a show during halftime of a football game.

Part A During one part of the show, the band members stand in 22 rows with 9 people in each row. Write an expression that shows how many band members there are in all. Then find the value of the expression.

Answer _____

Part B Use rounding to estimate the answer to part A. Is your answer reasonable? Explain.

_____

_____

16 Cora and her parents are going to see a movie. The tickets prices are shown below.

Adult	$10
Child (under 16)	$ 7
Seniors (60+)	$ 9

Part A Cora is under 16 and both of her parents are in their forties. What is the total cost of the family's tickets? Write an expression to represent the problem and then solve.

Answer _____

Part B Cora's grandmother, who is 67, decides that she would like to see the movie, too. If Cora's father has $40, does he have enough to pay for all four people? Explain.

_____

_____

Fractions

- **Lesson 1 Equivalent Fractions** reviews how to identify and find equivalent fractions using models and multiplication.

- **Lesson 2 Comparing Fractions** reviews how to compare two fractions with different numerators and denominators.

- **Lesson 3 Adding and Subtracting Fractions** reviews how to add and subtract fractions with like denominators, and how to decompose a fraction.

- **Lesson 4 Adding and Subtracting Mixed Numbers** reviews how to add and subtract mixed numbers with like denominators.

- **Lesson 5 Multiplying a Fraction by a Whole Number** reviews how to multiply a fraction by a whole number, using models and equations.

- **Lesson 6 Word Problems with Fractions** reviews how to solve word problems that involve adding and subtracting fractions or multiplying a fraction by a whole number.

Equivalent Fractions

4.NF.1

Equivalent fractions name the same number in different terms.

$$\frac{1}{2} = \frac{2}{4} \leftarrow \textbf{Numerator} \atop \leftarrow \textbf{Denominator}$$

The numerator and denominator are the **terms** of the fraction.

When the numerator and denominator are the same digit, the fraction is equal to 1.

$$\frac{2}{2} = 1$$

When you multiply or divide by 1, the number stays the same. So when you multiply or divide by $\frac{2}{2}$, you are only changing the terms.

Cross multiply to check if two fractions are equivalent. If the products are the same, the fractions are equivalent.

$$\frac{1}{4} = \frac{2}{8}$$
$$1 \times 8 = 4 \times 2$$
$$8 = 8$$

If $\frac{a}{b} = \frac{c}{d}$ and b, $d \neq 0$, then $ad = bc$.

Equivalent fractions are different fractions that have the same value. They show the same part of a whole in different ways.

You can use models to find equivalent fractions.

Nestor made a pan of brownies and cut it into 8 pieces of equal size. Then he ate 2 pieces. What fraction of the pan of brownies did Nestor eat?

To find the part Nestor ate, you can draw a model.

Draw a square divided into 8 pieces of equal size. Then, shade the pieces out of 8 that Nestor ate.

So, Nestor ate $\frac{2}{8}$ of the pan of brownies.

Look at the diagram again. Another way to describe the amount Nestor ate is 1 out of 4 parts, or $\frac{1}{4}$ of the pan.

You can also find equivalent fractions by multiplying or dividing. Multiply the numerator and denominator by the same number.

Multiply $\frac{1}{4}$ by $\frac{2}{2}$ to find an equivalent fraction in higher terms.

$$\frac{1}{4} \times \frac{2}{2} = \frac{1 \times 2}{4 \times 2} = \frac{2}{8}$$

Divide $\frac{4}{6}$ by $\frac{2}{2}$ to find an equivalent fraction in lower terms.

$$\frac{4}{6} \div \frac{2}{2} = \frac{4 \div 2}{6 \div 2} = \frac{2}{3}$$

SAMPLE Which of these fractions is equivalent to $\frac{1}{2}$?

A $\frac{3}{4}$ B $\frac{2}{2}$ C $\frac{2}{4}$ D $\frac{1}{4}$

> ✓ The correct answer is C. You can multiply the numerator and denominator of $\frac{1}{2}$ by the same number to find an equivalent fraction. The only answer choice that can be made is $\frac{2}{4}$ by multiplying $\frac{1}{2}$ by $\frac{2}{2}$: $\frac{1}{2} \times \frac{2}{2} = \frac{2}{4}$.

1 Maple trees make up $\frac{2}{5}$ of the trees in a park. Which of these fractions is equivalent to $\frac{2}{5}$?

A $\frac{2}{5}$ C $\frac{8}{5}$

B $\frac{4}{10}$ D $\frac{8}{10}$

2 Three-fourths of the people on a train are going to work. Which of these fractions is **_not_** equivalent to $\frac{3}{4}$?

A $\frac{9}{12}$ C $\frac{6}{8}$

B $\frac{3}{8}$ D $\frac{75}{100}$

3 Gabby feeds her hamster $\frac{1}{6}$ cup of food each day. Which fraction is equivalent to $\frac{1}{6}$?

A $\frac{2}{12}$ C $\frac{7}{12}$

B $\frac{3}{8}$ D $\frac{1}{12}$

4 Usher swims $\frac{4}{10}$ mile. What fraction of a mile could his brother swim in order to swim the same distance?

A $\frac{6}{12}$ C $\frac{4}{5}$

B $\frac{2}{8}$ D $\frac{2}{5}$

5 Which pair of fractions are equivalent?

A $\frac{1}{3}$ and $\frac{3}{6}$ C $\frac{2}{4}$ and $\frac{1}{3}$

B $\frac{2}{6}$ and $\frac{1}{3}$ D $\frac{6}{8}$ and $\frac{8}{6}$

6 Which model shows a fraction that is equivalent to $\frac{1}{3}$?

A   C

B   D

SAMPLE Ted and Todd have gardens of the same size. Ted plants vegetables in $\frac{3}{4}$ of his garden. Todd wants to plant vegetables in an equivalent area. What fraction of his garden should Todd plant with vegetables?

Ted's Garden   Todd's Garden

Answer _____

 Ted planted vegetables in $\frac{3}{4}$ of his garden. There are 12 sections in Todd's garden. To change $\frac{3}{4}$ to twelfths, multiply: $\frac{3}{4} \times \frac{3}{3} = \frac{9}{12}$. So, Todd will plant vegetables in 9 of the 12 sections, or $\frac{9}{12}$, of his garden.

7 What is a fraction equivalent to the shaded part of the model shown here?

Answer _____

8 Look at the fraction model here. Then draw and shade an equivalent fraction in the empty box. Name the equivalent fractions.

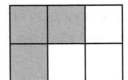 

Answer _____

9 Kerri runs $\frac{3}{4}$ mile. Her sister runs $\frac{5}{8}$ mile. Did they run equivalent distances? Explain how you know.

_____

_____

10 Emily wants to write a fraction equivalent to $\frac{1}{2}$. She wants to have a denominator of 100. What should she multiply the numerator and denominator of $\frac{1}{2}$ by? Explain.

_____

_____

UNIT 4 ▓▓▓▓▓▓▓▓▓▓▓▓▓▓▓▓▓▓▓▓▓▓▓▓▓▓▓▓▓▓▓▓▓
Fractions

11 Four students are using models to find fractions equivalent to $\frac{3}{10}$.

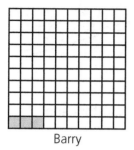
Barry

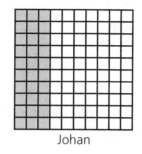
Johan

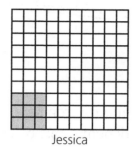
Jessica

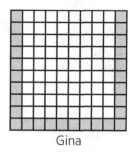
Gina

Part A Which student's model represents a fraction equivalent to $\frac{3}{10}$? Name that fraction.

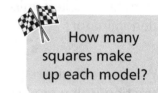
How many squares make up each model?

Answer _____

Part B Use multiplication to prove that the fraction your answer represents in part A and $\frac{3}{10}$ are equivalent. Show your work.

12 The table shows how much water four students drank today.

Student	Amount (in gallons)
Raj	$\frac{2}{3}$
Sue	$\frac{3}{5}$
Troy	$\frac{4}{6}$
Uma	$\frac{1}{2}$

Part A Which two students drank the same amount of water?

Answer _____

Part B Explain how you know your answer is correct.

_____

_____

LESSON 2

Comparing Fractions

4.NF.2

Different denominators are sometimes called **unlike** denominators.

When you compare fractions using models, be sure the wholes are the same size.

Common denominators are the same multiples of two or more numbers.

When fractions have the same numerator, just compare the denominators. The greater the denominator is, the smaller the fraction is.

$\frac{1}{3} < \frac{1}{2}$ because 3 > 2.

You can compare fractions with different numerators and denominators by using models.

Which fraction is greater, $\frac{2}{3}$ or $\frac{3}{4}$?

First, draw models of $\frac{2}{3}$ and $\frac{3}{4}$.

Next compare the shaded parts of each model.

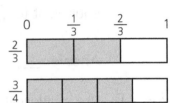

A greater part of the bottom model is shaded. So $\frac{3}{4} > \frac{2}{3}$.

You can also compare fractions by finding equivalent fractions with common denominators. Then compare the numerators. When two fractions have the same denominator, the fraction with the greater numerator is the greater fraction.

Which fraction is smaller, $\frac{2}{3}$ or $\frac{3}{4}$?

First, find a common denominator. List the multiples of each number.

Multiples of 3: 3, 6, 9, 12, …
Multiples of 4: 4, 8, 12, …

A common multiple is 12, so a common denominator of $\frac{2}{3}$ and $\frac{3}{4}$ is 12. Change each fraction to twelfths.

$$\frac{2}{3} \times \frac{4}{4} = \frac{8}{12} \qquad \frac{3}{4} \times \frac{3}{3} = \frac{9}{12}$$

Now compare the equivalent fractions. Look at the numerators.

$$\frac{8}{12} < \frac{9}{12}$$

Since 8 is less than 9, $\frac{2}{3} < \frac{3}{4}$.

SAMPLE Tabitha and Jane are competing in a swimming contest. Tabitha swims for $\frac{2}{5}$ mile. Jane swims for $\frac{1}{3}$ mile. Which number sentence is true?

A $\frac{2}{5} > \frac{1}{3}$ B $\frac{2}{5} < \frac{1}{3}$ C $\frac{2}{5} = \frac{1}{3}$ D $\frac{1}{3} > \frac{2}{5}$

The correct answer is A. A common denominator of 5 and 3 is 15. So $\frac{2}{5}$ is equivalent to $\frac{6}{15}$, and $\frac{1}{3}$ is equivalent to $\frac{5}{15}$. Compare: $\frac{6}{15} > \frac{5}{15}$, so $\frac{2}{5} > \frac{1}{3}$.

1 In one class, more than $\frac{3}{8}$ of the students play an instrument. Which could be the fraction of students who play an instrument?

A $\frac{1}{5}$ C $\frac{1}{3}$

B $\frac{1}{4}$ D $\frac{1}{2}$

2 Which number sentence is **not** true?

A $\frac{7}{12} < \frac{2}{3}$ C $\frac{7}{8} > \frac{3}{4}$

B $\frac{3}{6} < \frac{5}{12}$ D $\frac{7}{10} > \frac{3}{5}$

3 Lisa used less than $\frac{1}{3}$ of a stick of modeling clay. Which picture shows the amount Lisa could have used?

A 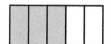   C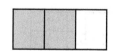

B    D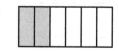

4 Henry bought less than $\frac{5}{8}$ kg of trail mix. Which fraction is less than $\frac{5}{8}$?

A $\frac{3}{4}$ C $\frac{7}{8}$

B $\frac{11}{12}$ D $\frac{1}{2}$

5 Which number sentence is true?

A $\frac{1}{3} < \frac{1}{4}$ C $\frac{9}{10} < \frac{9}{12}$

B $\frac{2}{5} < \frac{7}{10}$ D $\frac{3}{8} > \frac{3}{4}$

6 Paul draws a model of a fraction that is greater than $\frac{3}{4}$ but less than $\frac{9}{10}$. Which could be Paul's model?

A   C

B   D

SAMPLE Tina, Georgia, and Dave have the same amount of homework. Tina completes $\frac{2}{3}$ of her homework before dinner. Georgia completes $\frac{5}{8}$ of hers, and Dave completes $\frac{3}{4}$ of his. Write the students in order from most homework completed to least.

Answer _____

Change the fractions to equivalent fractions with the same denominator. A common denominator for 3, 8, and 4 is 24. So multiply to find Tina's fraction: $\frac{2}{3} \times \frac{8}{8} = \frac{16}{24}$. Multiply to find Georgia's fraction: $\frac{5}{8} \times \frac{3}{3} = \frac{15}{24}$. Multiply to find Dave's fraction: $\frac{3}{4} \times \frac{6}{6} = \frac{18}{24}$. Compare the numerators: $18 > 16 > 15$. From most homework completed to least, the students are Dave, Tina, Georgia.

7 Mei answered $\frac{3}{5}$ of the questions on a quiz correctly. Britt answered $\frac{5}{6}$ correctly, and Niel answered $\frac{2}{3}$ correctly. Write the fractions in order from least to greatest.

Answer _____

8 Ridge Trail is $\frac{3}{4}$ mile long. Valley Trail is $\frac{7}{12}$ mile long. Andrea wants to hike the longer trail. Which trail should she hike? Show your work.

Answer _____

9 Umberto believes the model shown here is greater than $\frac{3}{5}$. Is he correct? Explain your answer.

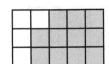

_____

_____

_____

10 Red, yellow, and blue are primary colors. Michael mixes equal parts of primary colors to make new colors. Michael mixes 2 parts blue and 1 part yellow to make green. He mixes 1 part red and 2 parts yellow to make orange.

Part A Which color, green or orange, is less than $\frac{3}{6}$ yellow? Explain your answer.

_____

_____

_____

_____

_____

The fractional size of a part depends on the number of equal parts in the whole. If there are 3 equal parts, then the parts represent $\frac{1}{3}$'s.

Part B Draw and label models to show the mixes for green and orange. Label each part in the models with a letter for the color. (Use B for blue, R for red, and Y for yellow.)

Adding and Subtracting Fractions

4.NF.3.a, b

If the fractions have different denominators, you must first find a **common denominator**.

When you draw models of fractions to add or subtract, the models for each whole must be the same size. That way, the parts being added are the same size.

You can also use models to find a difference.

$$\frac{3}{4} - \frac{1}{4} = \frac{2}{4}$$

When you add or subtract fractions, the fractions must have the same denominator.

You can use models to find a sum or difference of fractions with the same denominator.

Find $\frac{1}{3} + \frac{1}{3}$.

First, draw and shade a model of each fraction.

$$\frac{1}{3} + \frac{1}{3} = \frac{2}{3}$$

Then add the shaded part of each model together and draw a model of the sum.

So, $\frac{1}{3} + \frac{1}{3} = \frac{2}{3}$.

When fractions have the same denominator, you can also find a sum or difference by adding or subtracting the numerators.

What is $\frac{3}{4} - \frac{1}{4}$?

Both $\frac{3}{4}$ and $\frac{1}{4}$ have the same denominator. You can find the difference by subtracting their numerators, 3 – 1, and using their common denominator, 4. Write the answer in lowest terms.

$$\frac{3}{4} - \frac{1}{4} = \frac{3-1}{4} = \frac{2}{4} = \frac{1}{2}$$

So, $\frac{3}{4} - \frac{1}{4} = \frac{1}{2}$.

SAMPLE Martin makes spice cookies. He adds $\frac{1}{8}$ teaspoon of cinnamon, $\frac{1}{8}$ teaspoon of allspice, and $\frac{1}{8}$ teaspoon of nutmeg. How much spice did Martin add altogether?

A 24 teaspoons

C $\frac{3}{24}$ teaspoon

B 3 teaspoons

D $\frac{3}{8}$ teaspoon

The correct answer is D. The denominators are the same, so just add the numerators to find the sum: $\frac{1}{8} + \frac{1}{8} + \frac{1}{8} = \frac{3}{8}$.

1 What is $\frac{9}{10} - \frac{6}{10}$?

A $\frac{3}{20}$

C $\frac{3}{0}$

B $\frac{15}{20}$

D $\frac{3}{10}$

2 Which number sentence is true?

A $\frac{1}{8} + \frac{5}{8} = \frac{6}{16}$

C $\frac{2}{5} + \frac{2}{5} = \frac{4}{25}$

B $\frac{3}{12} + \frac{7}{12} = \frac{10}{12}$

D $\frac{7}{10} + \frac{7}{10} = \frac{14}{20}$

3 Which expression equals $\frac{5}{12}$?

A $\frac{3}{6} + \frac{2}{6}$

C $\frac{11}{12} - \frac{6}{12}$

B $\frac{9}{12} - 4$

D $\frac{4}{11} + \frac{1}{1}$

4 What is the answer to $\frac{1}{5} + \frac{2}{5}$?

A $\frac{3}{5}$

C $\frac{1}{5}$

B $\frac{2}{5}$

D $\frac{5}{5}$

5 Which model does **not** show a true situation?

A

B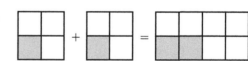

C

D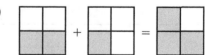

6 Which expression equals $\frac{7}{10}$?

A $\frac{9}{20} - \frac{2}{10}$

B $7 - \frac{0}{10}$

C $\frac{1}{10} + \frac{1}{10} + \frac{1}{10} + \frac{4}{10}$

D $\frac{1}{10} + \frac{2}{10} + \frac{3}{10} + 1$

SAMPLE Quinn is watching a science movie that is 1 hour long. Each scene in the movie lasts $\frac{1}{6}$ hour. How many scenes are there in the movie?

Answer _____

 Remember that 1 hour is the same as $\frac{6}{6}$ hour: $\frac{6}{6} = \frac{1}{6} + \frac{1}{6} + \frac{1}{6} + \frac{1}{6} + \frac{1}{6} + \frac{1}{6}$. So, there are six $\frac{1}{6}$-hour scenes in $\frac{6}{6}$ or 1 hour.

7 Tyrone wrote $\frac{1}{6}$ of his book report on Monday, $\frac{2}{6}$ on Tuesday, and another $\frac{1}{6}$ on Wednesday. How much of his report did Tyrone write by the end of Wednesday? Show your work.

Answer _____

8 Sonya wants to walk $\frac{8}{10}$ mile. She has already walked $\frac{3}{10}$ mile. How much farther does she have to walk to meet her goal? Explain how you found your answer.

_____

_____

_____

9 Vern believes he can completely fill the empty glass on the right using the liquid in the three glasses shown on the left. Is he correct? Explain your answer.

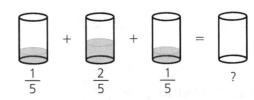

_____

_____

10 Lois is learning how to read musical notes. She has learned about whole notes, half notes, quarter notes, and eighth notes.

Part A Lois knows that 1 whole note is equal to 4 quarter notes. Write a number sentence that shows this.

The word *quarter* means "one-fourth." You can represent it using the fraction $\frac{1}{4}$.

Answer _____

Part B Lois believes there are the same number of eighth notes in a half note as there are quarter notes in a whole note. Is she correct? Explain how you got your answer and draw a model to prove it.

_____

_____

_____

_____

Adding and Subtracting Mixed Numbers

4.NF.3.c

A **mixed number** is made up of a whole number and a fraction.

$$2\frac{1}{2} = 2 + \frac{1}{2}$$

The associative property of addition allows you to group numbers in any way and the sum will be the same.

Always reduce fractions to lowest terms.

An **improper fraction** is a fraction with a numerator that is equal to or greater than its denominator, such as $\frac{5}{4}$.

To rewrite a mixed number as an improper fraction, multiply the denominator of the fraction by the whole number. Then add the numerator. Write the result over the denominator.

$$6\frac{1}{5} = \frac{(6 \times 5) + 1}{5} = \frac{31}{5}$$

You can add or subtract mixed numbers by adding or subtracting the fractions and then the whole numbers.

Topher biked $3\frac{3}{10}$ miles this morning and $2\frac{1}{10}$ miles this afternoon. How many miles did Topher bike altogether?

Find $3\frac{3}{10} + 2\frac{1}{10}$.

Write the mixed numbers as sums. $3 + \frac{3}{10} + 2 + \frac{1}{10}$

Add the fractions. $\frac{3}{10} + \frac{1}{10} = \frac{4}{10} = \frac{2}{5}$

Add the whole numbers. $3 + 2 = 5$

Then, add the sums together. $5 + \frac{2}{5} = 5\frac{2}{5}$

So, Topher biked $5\frac{2}{5}$ miles altogether.

Sometimes there are not enough fractional parts to subtract from. In that case, you can rename the mixed numbers as improper fractions.

Gary biked $6\frac{1}{5}$ miles. How many more miles did Gary bike than Topher?

Find $6\frac{1}{5} - 5\frac{2}{5}$.

You cannot subtract $\frac{2}{5}$ from $\frac{1}{5}$, so rename both mixed numbers as improper fractions.

$$6\frac{1}{5} = \frac{31}{5} \text{ and } 5\frac{2}{5} = \frac{27}{5}$$

Next, subtract the fractions. $\frac{31}{5} - \frac{27}{5} = \frac{4}{5}$

So, Gary biked $\frac{4}{5}$ mile more than Topher.

SAMPLE If it snowed $3\frac{2}{3}$ inches in December and $6\frac{1}{3}$ inches in January, how many inches did it snow during both months?

    A 10   **B** $9\frac{1}{3}$ **C** $3\frac{1}{3}$ **D** $2\frac{2}{3}$

The correct answer is A. To find the sum, add $3\frac{2}{3} + 6\frac{1}{3}$. First, add the fractions: $\frac{2}{3} + \frac{1}{3} = \frac{3}{3}$. Rewrite $\frac{3}{3}$ as 1, a whole number. Now, add the whole numbers: $3 + 6 + 1 = 10$. It snowed a total of 10 inches during both months.

1 Find the difference.

$$1\frac{6}{10} - 1\frac{3}{10} = \square$$

  A 3   **C** $\frac{9}{10}$

  B $1\frac{3}{10}$ **D** $\frac{3}{10}$

2 Add $2\frac{1}{8}$ and $3\frac{3}{8}$.

  A $5\frac{1}{2}$ **C** $1\frac{1}{2}$

  B $5\frac{1}{4}$ **D** $1\frac{1}{4}$

3 How much greater is $2\frac{3}{8}$ than $\frac{7}{8}$?

  A $3\frac{3}{8}$ **C** $1\frac{1}{2}$

  B $2\frac{1}{2}$ **D** $\frac{1}{2}$

4 Subtract:

$$14\frac{2}{5} - 2\frac{3}{5} = \square$$

  A $12\frac{1}{5}$ **C** $11\frac{4}{5}$

  B $12\frac{4}{5}$ **D** $11\frac{1}{5}$

5 Hilary needs to subtract $3\frac{4}{5}$ from $5\frac{1}{5}$. What improper fractions should she use?

  A $\frac{34}{5}$ and $\frac{51}{5}$ **C** $\frac{15}{5}$ and $\frac{25}{5}$

  B $\frac{7}{5}$ and $\frac{6}{5}$ **D** $\frac{19}{5}$ and $\frac{26}{5}$

6 Which number sentence is correct?

  A $1\frac{5}{6} + 4\frac{3}{6} = 5\frac{1}{2}$

  B $3\frac{1}{10} + 1\frac{9}{10} = 5$

  C $2\frac{1}{4} + 1\frac{3}{4} = 3$

  D $5\frac{2}{3} + 2\frac{2}{3} = 7\frac{1}{3}$

SAMPLE How can you subtract $9\frac{1}{5}$ from 12? Explain the steps you would take.

Answer _____

> The whole number 12 has no fractional part to subtract from. So, first change it to an improper fraction with a denominator of 5. Multiply: $5 \times 12 = 60$. Then write 60 over a denominator of 5: $\frac{60}{5}$. Next, change $9\frac{1}{5}$ to an improper fraction: $9\frac{1}{5} = \frac{5 \times 9 + 1}{5} = \frac{45 + 1}{5} = \frac{46}{5}$. Now, subtract: $\frac{60}{5} - \frac{46}{5} = \frac{14}{5}$. Finally, write the difference as a mixed number: $\frac{14}{5} = 2\frac{4}{5}$.

7 What is the sum of $2\frac{5}{6} + 2\frac{5}{6} + 2\frac{5}{6}$? Show your work.

Answer _____

8 Subtract $6\frac{1}{8} - 1\frac{7}{8}$. Show your work.

Answer _____

9 Dee added $2\frac{3}{4} + 3\frac{3}{4}$ this way:

$$2\frac{3}{4} + 3\frac{3}{4} = 2 + \frac{3}{4} + 3 + \frac{3}{4} = 2 + 3 + \frac{3}{4} + \frac{3}{4} = 5 + \frac{6}{4} = 5 + 1\frac{2}{4} = 6\frac{1}{2}$$

What property allowed Dee to break up the mixed numbers and rearrange them to add the whole numbers and fractions separately? Explain.

_____

_____

_____

10 Phillip plotted four points on a number line, as shown below.

Part A Which is greater, the difference between points A and B or the difference between points B and C? Show your work.

Answer _____

Part B Phillip added the values of points A and D this way:

$$\frac{7}{8} + 4\frac{7}{8} = 4 + \frac{7}{8} + \frac{7}{8} = 4 + \frac{14}{8} = 4\frac{6}{8} = 4\frac{3}{4}$$

What mistake did Phillip make? Explain and find the correct sum.

> What is an improper fraction? How do you change it to a mixed number?

_____

_____

_____

_____

Multiplying a Fraction by a Whole Number

4.NF.4.a, b

A fraction with a numerator of 1 is called a **unit fraction.**

When you multiply a unit fraction, $\frac{1}{x}$, by a whole number, a, the product can be a whole number or a mixed number. If the numerator is evenly divisible by the denominator, the result is a whole number.

Every whole number can be written as a fraction with a denominator of 1.

$$a = \frac{a}{1}$$

Reduce a fraction to lowest terms by dividing the numerator by the denominator.

You can multiply a fraction by a whole number using a model.

Find $4 \times \frac{1}{3}$.

Draw 4 squares. Divide each into thirds ($\frac{1}{3}$'s).

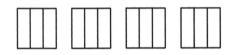

To find $4 \times \frac{1}{3}$, shade $\frac{1}{3}$ of each square.

$$4 \times \frac{1}{3} = \frac{4}{3} = 1\frac{1}{3}$$

Now find $3 \times \frac{2}{3}$. Think: $\frac{2}{3}$ is the same as $2 \times \frac{1}{3}$. So you can rewrite $3 \times \frac{2}{3}$ as $3 \times 2 \times \frac{1}{3}$ or $6 \times \frac{1}{3}$.

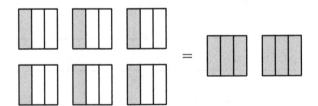

You can also multiply a fraction by a whole number using an equation.

What is $10 \times \frac{3}{5}$?

Write the whole number as a fraction with a denominator of 1. Then multiply the numerators. Multiply the denominators.

$$10 \times \frac{3}{5} = \frac{10}{1} \times \frac{3}{5} = \frac{10 \times 3}{1 \times 5} = \frac{30}{5} = 30 \div 5 = 6$$

SAMPLE Find $8 \times \frac{1}{5}$.

A $\frac{5}{8}$ **B** $\frac{1}{40}$ **C** $1\frac{3}{5}$ **D** 40

The correct answer is C. To find $8 \times \frac{1}{5}$, change 8 to an improper fraction, $\frac{8}{1}$. Multiply the numerators and multiply the denominators: $\frac{8 \times 1}{1 \times 5} = \frac{8}{5}$. Then divide the numerator by the denominator to write the fraction in lowest terms: $8 \div 5 = 1\frac{3}{5}$.

1 Which problem does the model represent?

A 4×5 **C** $5 \times \frac{1}{4}$

B $4 \times \frac{1}{5}$ **D** $5 \times \frac{1}{5}$

2 Find $9 \times \frac{1}{6}$.

A $\frac{6}{9}$ **C** $1\frac{1}{2}$

B $\frac{2}{3}$ **D** $\frac{1}{54}$

3 $16 \times \frac{1}{8}$ is 2. What is $16 \times \frac{5}{8}$?

A 8 **C** 40

B 10 **D** 80

4 Which expression is the same as $2 \times \frac{3}{4}$?

A $2 \times \frac{4}{3}$ **C** $8 \times \frac{1}{3}$

B $2 \times \frac{1}{4}$ **D** $6 \times \frac{1}{4}$

5 Multiply.

$$7 \times \frac{3}{7} = \square$$

A $\frac{1}{3}$ **C** 21

B 3 **D** 49

6 Find $8 \times \frac{3}{4}$.

A 6 **C** 12

B 8 **D** 24

7 Which expression is the same as $6 \times \frac{2}{3}$?

A $18 \times \frac{1}{2}$ **C** $6 \times \frac{3}{2}$

B $12 \times \frac{1}{3}$ **D** $6 \times \frac{1}{3}$

SAMPLE Find the product of $12 \times \frac{5}{6}$.

Answer _____

 You can use a shortcut to find the product of $12 \times \frac{5}{6}$. First multiply the whole number times the numerator of the fraction: $12 \times 5 = 60$. Then divide the result by the denominator: $\frac{60}{6} = 60 \div 6 = 10$. The product is 10.

8 $144 \times \frac{1}{12} = 12$. What is $144 \times \frac{5}{12}$?

Answer _____

9 Write an expression that is equivalent to $16 \times \frac{3}{8}$ using a unit fraction.

Answer _____

10 Find $9 \times \frac{7}{10}$. Show your work. Use the shortcut.

Answer _____

11 Explain how to use a model to find $24 \times \frac{1}{6}$.

_____

_____

_____

12 Jeanine knows that $25 \times \frac{1}{5}$ is 5.

Part A Jeanine says that $\frac{3}{5}$ is the same as $3 \times \frac{1}{5}$.
Is she correct? Draw models to prove your answer.

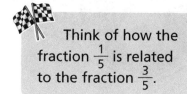

Think of how the fraction $\frac{1}{5}$ is related to the fraction $\frac{3}{5}$.

Answer _____

Part B How can Jeanine use what she knows to find $25 \times \frac{3}{5}$?
Explain.

_____

_____

_____

_____

Word Problems with Fractions

4.NF.3.d, 4.NF.4.c

You can use fractions to solve many kinds of word problems. Think carefully about the operation you need to use.

You can use a model to solve problems with fractions.

Remember that the denominator of the fractions is the number of parts your model should be divided into. The numerators of the fractions are the number of parts to shade.

An advertising agency rents $\frac{5}{12}$ of the offices in a building. A publishing company rents $\frac{3}{12}$ of the offices. Together, what fraction of the building's offices do the advertising agency and the publishing company rent?

To find a sum, add the two fractions. Divide a bar into 12 equal parts. Shade 5 parts to show the $\frac{5}{12}$. Shade 3 more parts to show the $\frac{3}{12}$.

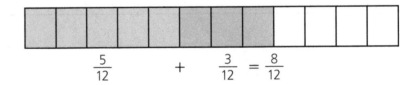

$$\frac{5}{12} \quad + \quad \frac{3}{12} \quad = \quad \frac{8}{12}$$

Together, the advertising agency and publishing company rent $\frac{8}{12}$ of the offices. In lowest terms, this is $\frac{2}{3}$ of the offices.

You can use an equation to solve problems with fractions.

Lawyers rent the rest of the offices in the building. What fraction of the offices do lawyers rent?

You can also use your bar model to find the fraction of offices rented by lawyers. You shaded 5 parts to show the fraction of offices rented by the advertising agency and 3 parts to show the fraction of offices rented by the publisher. The 4 unshaded parts of the bar show the $\frac{4}{12}$ of the offices that are rented by lawyers.

To find the fraction of the offices in the building rented by the lawyers, you need to subtract. Subtract the fraction of all the offices rented by the advertising agency and the publishing company, $\frac{8}{12}$, from the fraction that represents all the offices in the building, $\frac{12}{12}$.

$$\frac{12}{12} - \frac{8}{12} = \frac{4}{12}$$

Lawyers rent $\frac{4}{12}$ of the offices in the building.

SAMPLE Tauno makes 5 pecan pies. He uses $\frac{2}{3}$ cup brown sugar in each one. How much brown sugar does he use altogether?

A $\frac{10}{15}$ cup   **B** $2\frac{1}{3}$ cups   **C** $3\frac{1}{3}$ cups   **D** $5\frac{2}{3}$ cups

The correct answer is C. To combine equal amounts, you need to multiply. So multiply $\frac{2}{3}$ by 5: $5 \times \frac{2}{3} = \frac{5}{1} \times \frac{2}{3} = \frac{10}{3}$. Remember to change the improper fraction to a mixed number: $\frac{10}{3} = 10 \div 3 = 3$ R1 $= 3\frac{1}{3}$. Tauno uses $3\frac{1}{3}$ cups of brown sugar altogether.

1 Delilah bought a yard of satin ribbon. She cut off $\frac{4}{6}$ yard to decorate a package. What part of a yard does Delilah have left?

A $\frac{1}{6}$ **C** $\frac{1}{2}$

B $\frac{1}{3}$ **D** $\frac{2}{3}$

2 Two years ago, Anja grew $\frac{1}{12}$ foot. Last year, she grew another $\frac{4}{12}$ foot. This year she grew $\frac{2}{12}$ foot. How much did Anja grow in three years?

A $\frac{3}{12}$ foot   **C** $\frac{7}{12}$ foot

B $\frac{1}{2}$ foot   **D** 7 feet

3 The Lew family eats $\frac{3}{8}$ of a stew at dinner. They eat another $\frac{2}{8}$ of it at lunch the next day. How much of the stew is left?

A $\frac{7}{8}$ **C** $\frac{3}{8}$

B $\frac{5}{8}$ **D** $\frac{1}{8}$

4 In March, $3\frac{4}{10}$ inches of rain fell. In April, $4\frac{9}{10}$ inches of rain fell. How many more inches of rain fell in April than in March?

A $\frac{5}{10}$ **C** $1\frac{6}{10}$

B $1\frac{5}{10}$ **D** $8\frac{3}{10}$

5 A scientist does an experiment with 12 plants. He gives each plant exactly the same amount of water, $\frac{1}{5}$ liter. How much water does he give the plants in all?

A $\frac{1}{60}$ liter   **C** $2\frac{2}{5}$ liters

B $1\frac{2}{5}$ liters   **D** 12 liters

6 A lake is $5\frac{2}{5}$ miles long. Another nearby lake is $6\frac{4}{5}$ miles long. How much shorter is the first lake than the second lake?

A $1\frac{1}{5}$ miles   **C** $7\frac{3}{5}$ miles

B $1\frac{2}{5}$ miles   **D** $11\frac{2}{5}$ miles

SAMPLE Enzo has a part-time job. Last week, he worked $2\frac{3}{8}$ days. This week he worked $3\frac{7}{8}$ days. How many days did Enzo work at his part-time job in the past two weeks?

Answer _____

To find total time worked, add $2\frac{3}{8} + 3\frac{7}{8}$. First, add the whole numbers: $2 + 3 = 5$. Then add the fractions: $\frac{3}{8} + \frac{7}{8} = \frac{10}{8}$. Change the improper fraction to $1\frac{2}{8}$, or $1\frac{1}{4}$ in lowest terms. Finally, add the sums: $5 + 1\frac{1}{4} = 6\frac{1}{4}$. Enzo worked $6\frac{1}{4}$ days.

7 Eddie did jumping jacks for 3 minutes. Next, he jumped rope for $8\frac{1}{4}$ minutes. Then, he did chin-ups for $2\frac{1}{4}$ minutes. Eddie did not rest between exercises. How long did Eddie's workout take? Show your work.

Answer _____

8 A metal bar is $\frac{84}{100}$ inch long. A watchmaker trims $\frac{17}{100}$ inch from the end of the bar. How long is the trimmed bar? Write an equation to represent this problem and then solve it.

Answer _____

9 Karen walks a total of $\frac{3}{4}$ mile to and from school each day. How many miles does Karen walk in a week of 5 days? Draw and label a model on this number line to show this.

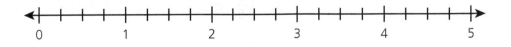

Answer _____

10 Mrs. Wright includes money in her budget for utilities. Utilities are things like electricity and phone service. In the average month, Mrs. Wright spends $\frac{3}{10}$ of the utilities money on electricity. She spends $\frac{4}{10}$ of it on gas to heat the house. She spends $\frac{1}{10}$ on water. The rest of the money goes to a company that provides cable, Internet, and phone service.

Part A What fraction of the utilities money does Mrs. Wright spend on electricity, gas, and water? Use the circle to model the answer.

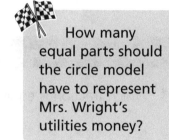

How many equal parts should the circle model have to represent Mrs. Wright's utilities money?

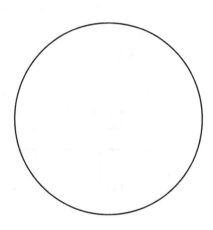

Explain how you found your answer.

_____

_____

_____

_____

Part B What fraction of the utilities money does Mrs. Wright spend on cable, Internet, and phone service? Explain how you found your answer.

_____

_____

_____

_____

UNIT 4
Fractions

95

REVIEW

Fractions

Read each problem. Circle the letter of the best answer.

1 Which fraction is equivalent to $\frac{6}{24}$?

A   C

B   D

2 What is the sum of $\frac{3}{8} + \frac{2}{8}$?

A $\frac{1}{8}$ C $\frac{2}{8}$

B $\frac{5}{8}$ D $\frac{6}{8}$

3 Which pair shows equivalent fractions?

A $\frac{1}{4}$ and $\frac{2}{6}$ C $\frac{2}{3}$ and $\frac{8}{12}$

B $\frac{3}{8}$ and $\frac{6}{12}$ D $\frac{3}{4}$ and $\frac{5}{8}$

4 Subtract $4\frac{1}{6} - \frac{5}{6}$.

A $3\frac{1}{3}$ C $4\frac{2}{3}$

B $3\frac{2}{3}$ D 5

5 A contractor pours more than $\frac{6}{10}$ of a sidewalk. Which model shows a fraction greater than $\frac{6}{10}$?

A  C

B  D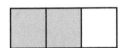

6 Which fraction is greater than $\frac{1}{3}$ and less than $\frac{3}{4}$?

A $\frac{1}{4}$ C $\frac{5}{6}$

B $\frac{2}{6}$ D $\frac{7}{12}$

7 Multiply $5 \times \frac{5}{10}$.

A $5\frac{1}{2}$ C $2\frac{2}{5}$

B $2\frac{1}{2}$ D $1\frac{1}{10}$

8 What is $\frac{9}{12} - \frac{4}{12}$?

Answer _____

9 Add $1\frac{5}{6} + 3\frac{2}{6}$. Show your work.

Answer _____

10 Find the product of $6 \times \frac{3}{8}$. Show your work.

Answer _____

11 At the deli, Chan Hee bought $\frac{3}{4}$ lb of American cheese. He also bought $\frac{3}{4}$ lb of Swiss cheese and $\frac{1}{4}$ lb of Jack cheese. How much cheese did Chan Hee buy?

Answer _____

12 Charlayne paddled $2\frac{3}{10}$ miles on the first day of a canoe trip. She paddled $4\frac{6}{10}$ miles on the second day. How much farther did Charlayne paddle the second day than the first day?

Answer _____

13 Mrs. Jenkins is buying pizza for the soccer team to eat after practice. Mrs. Jenkins estimates that each player will eat $\frac{3}{8}$ of a pizza.

Part A There are 17 players on the soccer team. If Mrs. Jenkins' estimate is correct, how much pizza will they eat? Show your work.

Answer _____

Part B Mrs. Jenkins orders 6 pizzas. If her estimate of how much pizza each player will eat is accurate, will there be enough pizza? Explain your answer.

_____

_____

_____

_____

Decimals

- **Lesson 1 Decimal Fractions** reviews how to express and add equivalent fractions with denominators of 10 and 100.

- **Lesson 2 Decimal Notation** reviews how to write decimal notation for fractions to the hundredths place.

- **Lesson 3 Comparing Decimals** reviews how to compare and order decimals to the hundredths place.

Decimal Fractions

4.NF.5

Equivalent fractions name the same value in different terms.

To add fractions, the denominators should be the same.

To find an equivalent fraction, multiply the numerator and denominator by the same number. A fraction with the same number in the numerator and denominator is equal to one.

$$\frac{10}{10} = 1$$

A fraction with a denominator of 10 can be **expressed,** or written, as an equivalent fraction with a denominator of 100.

You can use a model to find an equivalent fraction.

Express $\frac{3}{10}$ as an equivalent fraction.

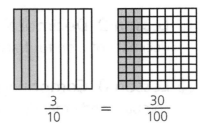

$$\frac{3}{10} \qquad = \qquad \frac{30}{100}$$

You can add two fractions with the unlike denominators 10 and 100.

$$\frac{2}{10} + \frac{6}{100} = \square$$

First, write $\frac{2}{10}$ as an equivalent fraction. Multiply $\frac{2}{10}$ by $\frac{10}{10}$.

$$\frac{2}{10} \times \frac{10}{10} = \frac{20}{100}$$
$$\frac{2}{10} = \frac{20}{100}$$

Now add the two fractions.

$$\frac{20}{100} + \frac{6}{100} = \frac{26}{100}$$

In a relay race, Linda swam $\frac{31}{100}$ kilometer and Shawn swam $\frac{4}{10}$ kilometer. What is the total distance they swam in the race?

$$\frac{4}{10} + \frac{31}{100} = \frac{40}{100} + \frac{31}{100} = \frac{71}{100}$$

They swam $\frac{71}{100}$ kilometer.

SAMPLE Which is an equivalent fraction to $\frac{6}{10}$?

    A $\frac{60}{10}$ **B** $\frac{10}{6}$ **C** $\frac{60}{100}$ **D** $\frac{6}{100}$

The correct answer is C. To find an equivalent fraction to $\frac{6}{10}$, multiply by $\frac{10}{10}$: $\frac{6}{10} \times \frac{10}{10} = \frac{60}{100}$. The fraction $\frac{6}{10}$ is equivalent to $\frac{60}{100}$.

1 Which fraction is equivalent to $\frac{7}{10}$?

  A $\frac{1}{7}$ **C** $\frac{7}{100}$

  B $\frac{70}{100}$ **D** $\frac{10}{700}$

2 Barney washes $\frac{5}{10}$ of the windows on a building. Which is an equivalent fraction to $\frac{5}{10}$?

  A $\frac{50}{100}$ **C** $\frac{5}{100}$

  B $\frac{500}{100}$ **D** $\frac{1}{5}$

3 Which is an equivalent fraction to $\frac{40}{100}$?

  A $\frac{4}{1}$ **C** $\frac{40}{10}$

  B $\frac{10}{40}$ **D** $\frac{4}{10}$

4 Which fraction is equivalent to $\frac{10}{100}$?

  A $\frac{10}{1}$ **C** $\frac{100}{10}$

  B $\frac{1}{10}$ **D** $\frac{1}{100}$

5 What is $\frac{3}{10} + \frac{15}{100}$?

  A $\frac{18}{10}$ **C** $\frac{18}{100}$

  B $\frac{45}{100}$ **D** $\frac{45}{10}$

6 Add:

$$\frac{7}{100} + \frac{2}{10} = \square$$

  A $\frac{9}{10}$ **C** $\frac{27}{100}$

  B $\frac{9}{100}$ **D** $\frac{72}{100}$

7 Find the sum of $\frac{4}{10} + \frac{59}{100}$.

  A $\frac{10}{99}$ **C** $\frac{63}{100}$

  B $\frac{63}{10}$ **D** $\frac{99}{100}$

8 Find the sum of $\frac{3}{100} + \frac{5}{10}$.

  A $\frac{35}{10}$ **C** $\frac{35}{100}$

  B $\frac{8}{10}$ **D** $\frac{53}{100}$

UNIT 5
Decimals

SAMPLE Lily wants to find the sum of $\frac{12}{100}$ and $\frac{8}{10}$. Explain the steps she needs to take.

> The fractions $\frac{12}{100}$ and $\frac{8}{10}$ have unlike, or different, denominators. To add the fractions, the denominators must be the same. So the first step Lily needs to take is to find the equivalent fraction for $\frac{8}{10}$ with the denominator 100 by multiplying: $\frac{8}{10} \times \frac{10}{10} = \frac{80}{100}$. Then she can add to find the sum.

9 Find the equivalent fraction for $\frac{9}{10}$ with the denominator 100. Explain your answer.

_____

_____

10 Explain why $\frac{3}{10}$ and $\frac{30}{100}$ have unlike denominators but are equivalent fractions.

_____

_____

_____

11 The library is $\frac{25}{100}$ kilometer from Nick's school and the track field is $\frac{3}{10}$ kilometer directly beyond the library. What is the total distance from the school to the track field? Explain how you found the total distance.

_____

_____

_____

12 Add $\frac{1}{10}$ and $\frac{1}{100}$. Show your work.

Answer _____

13 One Saturday, Frederic volunteered at the animal hospital in the morning and the park zoo in the afternoon.

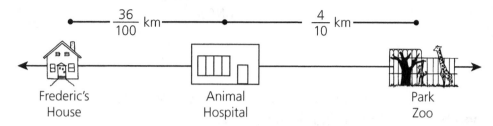

Part A Use the diagram. What is the total distance from Frederic's home to the park zoo?

Answer _____

Part B Explain how you found the total distance.

_____

_____

14 Dara, Eva, and Sanjay are running for student council. Dara received $\frac{32}{100}$ of the votes. Eva received $\frac{33}{100}$ of the votes. Sanjay received $\frac{3}{10}$ of the votes.

Part A What part of the votes did they receive together?

Answer _____

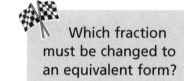

Which fraction must be changed to an equivalent form?

Part B Explain how you found the part of the votes.

_____

_____

Decimal Notation

4.NF.6

In **decimal notation**, numbers are written using place values.

Ones	Decimal point	Tenths	Hundredths
0	.	3	5

0.35

Each place has a value 10 times the place to its right. Each place has a value $\frac{1}{10}$ the place to its left.

1 tenth = 10 hundredths

Remember that tenths can be expressed as equivalent numbers in hundredths.

$$\frac{6}{10} = \frac{60}{100}$$

0.6 = 0.60

6 tenths = 60 hundredths

You can write fractions with denominators of 10 and 100 in standard form using **decimal notation**.

What are $\frac{6}{10}$ and $\frac{64}{100}$ in decimal notation?

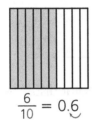

$$\frac{6}{10} = 0.6$$

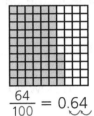

$$\frac{64}{100} = 0.64$$

Write the numerator. Look at the denominator and count the number of zeros. Place the decimal point the same number of places to the left. The fraction $\frac{6}{10}$ has one zero, so put the decimal point one place to the left. The fraction $\frac{64}{100}$ has two zeros, so put the decimal point two places to the left.

You can find decimals on a number line.

Randy and Felix are building bookcases. Randy's shelves are $\frac{78}{100}$ m long. Felix's shelves are $\frac{9}{10}$ m long. Find the decimals on the number line.

First, write decimal notation for the fractions.

$$\frac{78}{100} = 0.78 \qquad \frac{9}{10} = 0.9$$

Then find them on the number line.

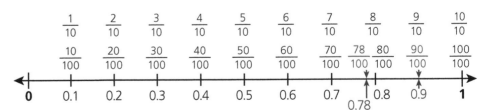

SAMPLE What is $\frac{23}{100}$ written as a decimal?

A 0.023 B 0.23 C 23 D 2,300

The correct answer is B. To find the decimal for $\frac{23}{100}$, first write the numerator 23. Then put a decimal point two places to the left because the denominator 100 has two zeros.

1 Joan drinks $\frac{7}{10}$ liter of water today. What is the decimal notation for $\frac{7}{10}$?

A 70 C 0.7

B 7 D 0.07

2 What fraction does 0.26 represent?

A $\frac{26}{100}$ C $\frac{26}{10}$

B $\frac{260}{100}$ D $\frac{1}{26}$

3 Which fraction is equal to the decimal marked by an arrow on the number line?

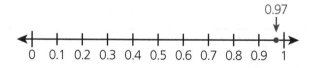

A $\frac{97}{10}$ C $\frac{1}{97}$

B $\frac{97}{100}$ D $\frac{10}{97}$

4 Which decimal is equal to $\frac{9}{100}$?

A 0.09 C 9

B 0.9 D 90

5 Which list shows equivalent fractions and decimals?

A $\frac{2}{1}, \frac{2}{10}, 2.0$ C $\frac{20}{10}, \frac{20}{100}, 0.2$

B $\frac{1}{20}, \frac{10}{200}, 0.20$ D $\frac{2}{10}, \frac{20}{100}, 0.2$

6 Which decimal is equal to the fraction marked by an arrow on the number line?

A 0.08 C 0.8

B 8.10 D 10.8

7 Helga puts 0.28 kilogram of grapes in a bag. Which fraction is equal to 0.28?

A $\frac{28}{10}$ C $\frac{280}{100}$

B $\frac{28}{100}$ D $\frac{10}{28}$

SAMPLE What are two decimal notations for the fraction $\frac{5}{10}$?

Answer _____

> The fraction $\frac{5}{10}$ is read "five tenths," so one decimal notation for it is 0.5. Write the numerator 5 and move the decimal point one place left. Since 5 tenths are equal to 50 hundredths, you can also write this number as 0.50. The decimals 0.5 and 0.50 name the same number.

8 What is the decimal notation for the fraction $\frac{3}{10}$?

Answer _____

9 What fraction with a denominator of 100 is equivalent to $\frac{3}{10}$? What is the decimal notation for this fraction?

Answer _____

10 Explain how to write the fraction $\frac{57}{100}$ in decimal notation.

_____

_____

11 Beth wrote the fraction $\frac{5}{100}$ as 0.5. Brandon wrote the same fraction as 0.05. Who is correct? Explain how you know.

_____

_____

12 Change the fractions $\frac{43}{100}$ and $\frac{7}{10}$ to decimals. Then find and mark them on the number line below.

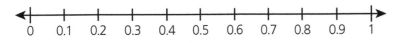

(106) **UNIT 5** ▓▓
Decimals

13 Look at this model.

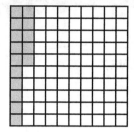

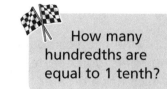

How many hundredths are equal to 1 tenth?

Part A Write a fraction with a denominator of 100 and a decimal to represent the number shown on the model.

Answer _____

Part B Can you write this number as an equivalent fraction or decimal in tenths? Explain your answer.

_____

_____

_____

14 Lars and Gwen each make a nutrition poster.

Part A Lars' poster measures $\frac{8}{10}$ m tall and $\frac{5}{10}$ m wide. What is the decimal notation for each fraction? Find and mark the decimals on the number line below.

Answer _____

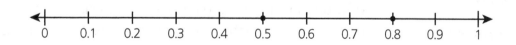

Part B Gwen's poster measures $\frac{76}{100}$ m tall and $\frac{45}{100}$ m wide. What is the decimal notation for each fraction? Find and mark the decimals on the number line below.

Answer _____

```
◄──┼───┼───┼───┼───┼───┼───┼───┼───┼───┼──►
   0  0.1 0.2 0.3 0.4 0.5 0.6 0.7 0.8 0.9  1
```

Comparing Decimals

4.NF.7

When you compare numbers, you decide which has a greater value.

You can also compare decimals the same way you do whole numbers. Compare the digits in the same places: tenths to tenths, and hundredths to hundredths.

0.75 > 0.60
because
7 tenths >
6 tenths

You can compare numbers in number sentences using these symbols:

< means "is less than"
> means "is greater than"
= means "is equal to"

When you **order** numbers, you arrange them in order of size from least to greatest or greatest to least.

Numbers to the left on a number line are always less than numbers to the right.

When two decimals represent parts of the same whole, you can compare them.

You can compare decimals using area models.

Compare 0.75 and 0.60.

Two 100-square grids of the same size can be used to compare the two decimals. In the grid on the left, shade 75 squares to represent 0.75. In the grid on the right, shade 60 squares.

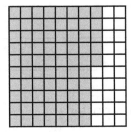 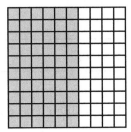

Then compare. The shaded area for 0.75 is greater than the shaded area for 0.60.

0.75 > 0.60

You can compare and order decimals using a number line.

Carrie, Liz, and Nathan picked blueberries. Carrie picked 0.76 pound, Liz picked 0.86 pound, and Nathan picked 0.51 pound of blueberries. Order the weights from least to greatest, using the symbols >, =, or <.

Locate and label each weight on the number line.

The number line shows that 0.51 is less than 0.76, and 0.76 is less than 0.86. Write a number sentence with symbols to show this.

0.51 < 0.76 < 0.86

SAMPLE Which decimal is greater than 0.28?

    A 0.09   **B** 0.19   **C** 0.27   **D** 0.3

> The correct answer is D. Choice A is incorrect because 0 tenths is less than 2 tenths. Choice B has 1 in the tenths place, so it is incorrect. Choice C has 2 tenths and 7 hundredths, which is less than 2 tenths 8 hundredths. So it is incorrect. Choice D is correct because 3 tenths are greater than 2 tenths.

1 More than 3.78 meters of ribbon are left on a roll. Which decimal could be the amount left on the roll?

    A 3.81 meters   **C** 2.99 meters

    B 3.69 meters   **D** 2.89 meters

2 Which comparison is true?

    A 0.19 > 0.21   **C** 0.36 > 0.27

    B 0.29 < 0.27   **D** 0.82 < 0.78

3 Which shows decimals in order from least to greatest?

    A 0.05, 0.12, 1.01

    B 1.05, 1.55, 0.05

    C 0.99, 1.99, 1.09

    D 1.88, 1.08, 1.18

4 Which decimal is less than 0.4?

    A 1.02   **C** 0.4

    B 0.42   **D** 0.09

5 Which comparison is **not** true?

    A 1.03 > 0.95   **C** 1.2 = 1.20

    B 1.31 < 0.91   **D** 0.08 < 0.09

6 Astrid marked two decimals on this number line.

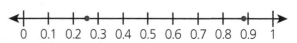

Which decimals could they be?

    A 0.2 and 0.8

    B 0.35 and 0.91

    C 0.36 and 0.88

    D 0.26 and 0.89

7 Huberto has 0.07 kg of walnuts, 0.31 kg of almonds, and 0.65 kg of peanuts. Which shows these amounts in order from greatest to least?

    A 0.07, 0.31, 0.65

    B 0.65, 0.31, 0.07

    C 0.65, 0.07, 0.31

    D 0.07, 0.65, 0.31

SAMPLE Fay ate 0.4 pound of cherries. Neela ate 0.46 pound of cherries. Kate ate an amount between Fay and Neela's amounts. Write a decimal that could name the amount of cherries Kate ate.

Answer _____

You need to find a number that is greater than 0.4 and less than 0.46. To make it easier, change 0.4 to hundredths: 0.40. Now find a decimal greater than 0.40 but not greater than 0.46: 0.41, 0.42, 0.43, 0.44, 0.45. These could all be amounts that Kate ate.

8 Three 1-liter pitchers contain lemonade. Pitcher A has 0.68 liter. Pitcher B has 0.84 liter. Pitcher C has 0.72 liter. Which pitcher has the greatest amount of lemonade? Explain how you know.

_____

_____

9 Edward buys three items. He pays $0.65, $0.99, $0.49. Order the prices from least to greatest.

Answer _____

10 Mark and label the decimals 0.52, 0.2, 0.02 on the number line below. Then order the decimals from least to greatest using >, =, or < symbols.

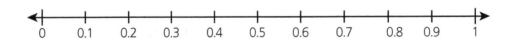

Answer _____

11 Is 0.5 greater than or less than 0.39? Use the grids to model the numbers and prove your answer.

Answer _____

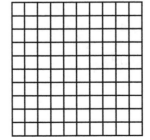
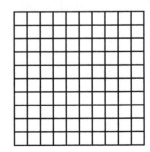

12 Three trucks haul rocks from a quarry. Truck A carries 0.57 ton.
Truck B carries 0.65 ton. Truck C carries 0.09 ton.

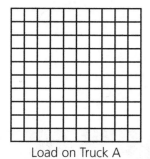
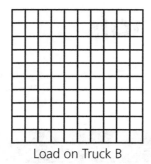
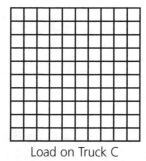

Load on Truck A   Load on Truck B   Load on Truck C

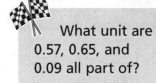

What unit are
0.57, 0.65, and
0.09 all part of?

Part A Shade the weights on the grids. Explain why you can
compare these decimals.

_____

_____

Part B Amir ordered the load weights on each truck from least to
greatest as follows: 0.57 ton, 0.65 ton, and 0.09 ton. What
mistake did Amir make? Explain. Write the correct order
using the symbols <, =, or >.

_____

_____

_____

_____

REVIEW

Decimals

Read each problem. Circle the letter of the best answer.

1 Francine read $\frac{3}{10}$ of the books in a series. Which fraction is equivalent to $\frac{3}{10}$?

A $\frac{1}{3}$　　C $\frac{30}{100}$

B $\frac{3}{1}$　　D $\frac{300}{100}$

2 Add $\frac{4}{10} + \frac{34}{100}$.

A $\frac{38}{10}$　　C $\frac{74}{10}$

B $\frac{38}{100}$　　D $\frac{74}{100}$

3 A truck carried $\frac{81}{100}$ ton of sand. What is the decimal notation for $\frac{81}{100}$?

A　0.081　　C　8.1

B　0.81　　D　81

4 Carson lives more than 4.67 kilometers from the baseball stadium. Which decimal is greater than 4.67?

A　4.09　　C　4.49

B　4.71　　D　4.59

5 Which fraction is equal to the decimal marked by the arrow on the number line?

A $\frac{5}{100}$　　C $\frac{1}{10}$

B $\frac{1}{100}$　　D $\frac{5}{10}$

6 What decimal names $\frac{5}{10}$?

A　50　　C　0.5

B　5　　D　0.05

7 Which comparison is true?

A　0.28 > 0.29　　C　0.26 > 0.19

B　0.28 < 0.27　　D　0.19 > 0.26

8 Levi buys 0.83 lb of seed corn and 0.33 lb of bean seeds. He also buys 0.03 lb of flower seeds. Which shows these decimals in order from least to greatest?

A　0.03, 0:33, 0.83　C　0.83, 0.33, 0.03

B　0.33, 0.03, 0.83　D　0.83, 0.03, 0.33

9 Find the equivalent fraction for $\frac{2}{10}$ with the denominator 100.
Show your work.

Answer _____

10 The camp cabin is $\frac{38}{100}$ kilometer from the boat dock. The campfire
circle is $\frac{2}{10}$ kilometer behind the cabins in the opposite direction. What
is the total distance from the boat dock to the campfire circles? Explain
how you found the total distance.

_____

_____

11 What is the decimal notation for the fraction $\frac{7}{10}$?

Answer _____

12 What fraction with the denominator 100 is equivalent to $\frac{7}{10}$? What is
the decimal notation for this fraction?

Answer _____

13 Elton builds a 3-D puzzle that is $\frac{48}{100}$ m tall. The display case for it is
$\frac{6}{10}$ m tall. Change each measure to a decimal. Then find and mark the
decimals on the number line below.

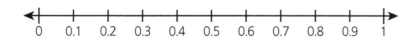

14 A science experiment uses 0.82 liter, 0.69 liter, and 0.74 liter of three
different liquids. Compare and order the amounts from greatest to
least using the symbols <, =, or >.

Answer _____

15 Valerie thinks the decimals 0.9, 0.09, and 0.90 all represent the same fraction.

Part A On the grids below, represent each decimal. Label each model with the decimal it stands for.

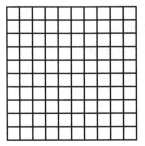   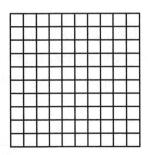   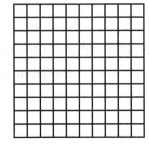

_____   _____   _____

Part B What fraction does each decimal represent? Explain how you know.

_____

_____

_____

16 The table at the right shows the typical weights of some breeds of horses.

WEIGHTS OF HORSES

Breed	Weight
Clydesdale	0.75 ton
Quarter horse	0.49 ton
Shetland pony	0.27 ton

Part A Chandler ordered the weights from least to greatest this way: 0.27 ton, 0.75 ton, and 0.49 ton. Explain Chandler's mistake. Then write the correct order using the symbols < or >.

_____

_____

Part B A Clydesdale horse is very tall. A person riding a Clydesdale can be 1.78 meters above the ground. Can the decimals for this distance and the Clydesdale's weight be compared? Explain your answer.

_____

_____

Patterns

- **Lesson 1 Number Patterns** reviews how to recognize a number pattern and identify the rule. It also reviews how to find a missing number and to create a number pattern given the rule.

- **Lesson 2 Shape Patterns** reviews how to recognize a shape pattern, describe the rule, find a missing shape, and create a shape pattern from given information.

Number Patterns

4.OA.5

A **number pattern** is a sequence of numbers that follows a rule.

What is the rule for this number pattern?

1, 5, 9, 13, 17, 21

Study the numbers to find how they are changing. First, the numbers are increasing. The number 5 is 4 greater than 1. Each new number is 4 greater than the number before it. Check that this true for every number in the pattern.

$1 + 4 = 5$ $5 + 4 = 9$ $9 + 4 = 13$

$13 + 4 = 17$ $17 + 4 = 21$

The rule is "add 4."

Once you know the rule, you can find the next number in the pattern.

What number comes next in the sequence above?

To find the next number, apply the rule. The last number in the pattern is 21. Add 4 to that number: $21 + 4 = 25$. The next number in the pattern is 25.

You can use a rule and a starting number to make a pattern of numbers.

The rule is "add 5." The starting number is 12. What are the first six numbers in this pattern?

Apply the rule to the starting number: $12 + 5 = 17$. The second number in the pattern is 17.

Continue to apply the rule to each new number.

$17 + 5 = 22$ $22 + 5 = 27$ $27 + 5 = 32$ $32 + 5 = 37$

The first six numbers in the pattern are 12, 17, 22, 27, 32, 37.

A pattern can be found in sequences of numbers or shapes. Some patterns repeat.

A B A B A B

Other patterns grow.

1, 2, 4, 8

A number pattern is not just a set or group of numbers. The **sequence,** or order, the numbers are in is an important part of the pattern.

A number pattern may have features that are not spelled out in the rule.

Notice that the pattern 1, 5, 9, 13, 17, 21 includes only odd numbers. The rule for the pattern is "add 4." If you start with 1 and add 4 repeatedly, all the numbers generated will be odd. This is because 1 is an odd number, and 4 is an even number. If the pattern had started with an even number, such as 2, all the numbers in the pattern would be even.

SAMPLE What is the next number in this pattern?

77, 66, 56, 47, 39, __?__

A 34   **B** 32   **C** 31   **D** 30

The correct answer is B. The numbers decrease but by a different amount every time.

77 − 66 = 11
66 − 56 = 10
56 − 47 = 9
47 − 39 = 8

Each new number is decreased by a number that is 1 less than the number before it was decreased. So, the next number will be decreased by 7: 39 − 7 = 32.

1 What is the rule?

97, 87, 77, 67, 57, 47, 37

A add 1   **C** subtract 1

B add 10   **D** subtract 10

2 What is the rule?

2, 4, 8, 16, 32, 64, 128

A add 2   **C** multiply by 2

B add 4   **D** multiply by 4

3 The rule is "add 6." The start number is 18. What are the first six numbers in the pattern?

A 1, 6, 12, 18, 24, 30

B 18, 26, 36, 46, 56, 66

C 6, 12, 18, 24, 30, 36

D 18, 24, 30, 36, 42, 48

4 What is the next number in the pattern?

876, 765, 654, 543, 432, __?__

A 231   **C** 321

B 312   **D** 331

5 Arlene creates a pattern using the rule "subtract 3." She starts with 45. What will be true of the numbers in this pattern?

A They will all be odd.

B They will all be even.

C They will all be multiples of 5.

D They will all be multiples of 3.

6 What is the missing number in this pattern?

2, 5, __?__, 14, 20, 27, 35

A 6   **C** 9

B 8   **D** 11

SAMPLE What is the next number in this pattern?

1, 1, 2, 3, 5, 8, 13, 21, _____

Answer _____

✔ To get each new number in the pattern, you add the two numbers that come before it. That is the rule: 1 + 1 = 2, 1 + 2 = 3, 2 + 3 = 5, 3 + 5 = 8, 5 + 8 = 13, 8 + 13 = 21. So, the next number is 13 + 21 = 34.

7 The rule is "subtract 3." The start number is 127. What is the 10th number in the pattern?

Answer _____

8 Tucker builds a pattern using the rule "add 5." He starts with the number 4. What will be true of the numbers in the pattern? Explain why the pattern has that feature.

_____

_____

_____

_____

9 What is the rule for this pattern?

195, 285, 375, 465, 555, 645

Answer _____

10 Yelena is able to run 8 miles. She trains so that each week she is able to run 2 more miles than she could the week before. How many weeks of training does it take for her to be able to run a 26-mile marathon?

Answer _____

11 Ivan arranges a display of cans of peaches at the grocery store. Only the top three rows are shown below.

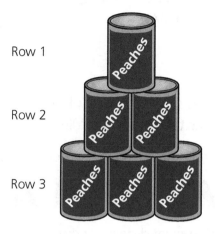

Row 1

Row 2

Row 3

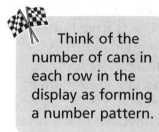

Think of the number of cans in each row in the display as forming a number pattern.

Part A There are 17 rows of cans in all. The rows follow the pattern shown in the picture above. How many cans are in the bottom row? Explain how you know.

_____

_____

_____

Part B How many cans are in the entire display? Show your work.

Answer _____

Shape Patterns

4.OA.5

A shape pattern uses shapes instead of numbers. Like a number pattern, a **shape pattern** follows a rule.

Describe the rule for the shape pattern below.

Look at the shapes and decide how they change. The direction they point changes: up, right, down, left. Then the pattern starts to repeat. The rule is "rotate a quarter turn clockwise."

Once you know the rule, you can predict the next shape.

What is the next shape in the pattern above?

To find the next shape, apply the rule. The last triangle in the pattern points right. The rule is "rotate a quarter turn clockwise." So, the next triangle points down.

You can use a rule to create a shape pattern.

The rule is "alternate square, circle, triangle, and also alternate white and black." Start with a white square. Identify the first five shapes in the pattern.

Begin by drawing the first five shapes in order: square, circle, triangle, and then repeat square, circle.

Now, alternate white and black, starting with a white square.

Those are the first five shapes in the pattern.

SAMPLE What is the next shape in this pattern?

A   B   C   D

 The correct answer is C. Sometimes the shape itself changes in a pattern. The rule here is that the number of points of each star increases by 1. The last star in the pattern has 6 points, so the next star will have 7 points. Choice A has 12 points. Choice B has 8 points. Choice D does have 7 points but, unlike the stars in the pattern, it is not solid black.

1 What is the rule?

A   alternate white and black

B   black, blue, white, black

C   white, blue, white, black

D   blue, then white, then black

2 What is the rule?

A   add 4 hours   **C**   subtract 5 hours

B   add 7 hours   **D**   subtract 7 hours

3 What is the next letter in the pattern?

ABBACCADDA

A **B**   C **D**

B **C**   D **E**

4 What is the next shape in this pattern?

A   C

B   D

5 The rule is "rotate a half turn." Start with an arrow pointing left. What are the first five shapes in the pattern?

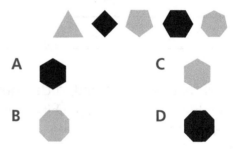

SAMPLE What shape is missing in the pattern?

Answer _____

 First identify the pattern and find where the repeat begins. The pattern starts with a plus sign, a minus sign, a plus sign, a times sign, and then the pattern begins to repeat. The missing shape is the third sign in the pattern, a plus sign.

6 Describe the rule for this pattern.

_____

_____

7 The rule is "alternate diamond, circle, square, triangle, and alternate white and black." Start with a white diamond. What is the 12th shape in the pattern?

Answer _____

8 Draw the shape pattern described in problem 7 to the 16th figure.

Answer _____

9 Amanda says the shapes in the pattern in problem 7 will always be the same color. Is she correct? (Hint: Think about factors.) Explain.

_____

_____

_____

10 The rule is "alternate diamond, square, and circle, and also alternate white and black."

Part A   Start with a white diamond and draw the pattern below.

Draw the shapes first, in the order named. Then apply the other part of the rule to color the shapes.

What is the 11th shape in the pattern?

Answer _____

Part B   Does the pattern ever repeat? If so, how many unique shapes are there before the pattern repeats? Explain.

_____

_____

_____

_____

REVIEW

Patterns

Read each problem. Circle the letter of the best answer.

1 What is the rule?

486, 162, 54, 18, 6, 2

A subtract 324 **C** multiply by 3

B divide by 2 **D** divide by 3

2 What is the rule?

A Rotate a half-turn.

B Rotate a quarter-turn clockwise.

C Rotate a quarter-turn counterclockwise.

D Rotate a three-quarter-turn clockwise.

3 The rule is "multiply by 2." The start number is 2. What are the first six numbers in the pattern?

A 2, 4, 8, 16, 32, 64

B 2, 4, 6, 8, 10, 12

C 2, 4, 8, 12, 24, 48

D 8, 16, 13, 26, 23, 46

4 What is the next shape in this pattern?

A ● **C** ■

B ○ **D** □

5 What is the next number in this pattern?

78, 69, 60, 51, 42, 33, ___?___

A 22 **C** 24

B 23 **D** 29

6 Owen creates a pattern using the rule "add 10." He starts with the number 7. What will be true of the numbers in the pattern?

A They will all have a 0 in the ones place.

B They will all have a 7 in the ones place.

C They will be multiples of 10.

D They will all be multiples of 7.

7 What is the rule?

957, 887, 817, 747, 677, 607

Answer _____

8 The rule is "add 4." The start number is 39. What are the first six numbers in the pattern?

Answer _____

9 Lamont says the pattern in problem 8 will always result in an odd number. Is he correct? Explain how you know.

_____

_____

_____

10 The rule is "alternate circle, square, triangle, star, and also alternate black and white." Start with a black circle. What is the 15th shape in the pattern?

Answer _____

11 Every two weeks, Jeff buys a pack of 10 trading cards. He started with 58 trading cards. How many weeks will it take Jeff to reach 100 trading cards? Show your work.

Answer _____

12 Portia designs this pattern to decorate her bedroom wall.

Part A What is the 14th shape in Portia's pattern?

Answer _____

Part B Portia decides to alternate the shapes in red and yellow. She starts with red. Does the new pattern ever repeat? If so, how many unique shapes are there before the pattern repeats? Explain.

_____

_____

_____

_____

Measurement

● **Lesson 1 Customary Units of Measurement** reviews customary units of length, weight, capacity, and units of time.

● **Lesson 2 Metric Units of Measurement** reviews metric units of length, mass, and capacity.

● **Lesson 3 Measurement Conversions** reviews how to change measurements in units of one size into units of a different size within a given measurement system.

● **Lesson 4 Measurement Word Problems** reviews how to solve multi-step problems involving measurements.

● **Lesson 5 Measurement Data** reviews how to solve problems involving measurement information in line plots.

UNIT 7
Measurement
127

Customary Units of Measurement

4.MD.1

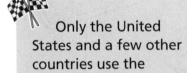

Only the United States and a few other countries use the customary system.

Units such as the inch and foot were originally related to the lengths of body parts. In many languages, the word for *inch* is the same as the word for *thumb*.

Units of capacity are used to measure things besides liquids. Loose things that flow, like sugar, rice, or flour, are often measured this way.

Choose the most appropriate unit when measuring. Always measure objects using the smallest whole number possible. Use larger units for larger objects and smaller units for smaller objects.

The **customary system** is used to measure length, capacity, weight, and time.

Units of **length** measure how long, wide, tall, or deep something is.

inch (in.)	The length of a pushpin is about 1 inch.
foot (ft)	A water bottle is about 1 foot tall.
yard (yd)	The width of a door is about 1 yard.
mile (mi)	The combined height of 4 Empire State Buildings is about 1 mile.

Units of **capacity** measure how much liquid is in a container.

cup (C)	A mug holds about 1 cup.
pint (pt)	A small ice cream carton holds about 1 pint.
quart (qt)	A large water bottle holds about 1 quart.
gallon (gal)	A large plastic milk jug holds 1 gallon.

Units of **weight** measure how heavy something is.

ounce (oz)	A house mouse weighs about 1 ounce.
pound (lb)	A soccer ball weighs about 1 pound.

Which unit would be most appropriate to measure the depth of snow that falls in an hour?

Depth is a type of length. You can measure the depth of snow with a ruler. Usually only a small amount of snow falls in an hour, so inches are the best unit to use.

Units of time measure how long something lasts.

second (sec)	Clapping your hands once takes about 1 second.
minute (min)	A short e-mail takes about 1 minute to write.
hour (hr)	A TV show lasts about 1 hour.

Which unit would be best to measure how long it takes to walk a mile?

Most people can walk about 3 miles in 1 hour, so a smaller distance, 1 mile, would be measured using smaller units, minutes. Most people walk 1 mile in about 20 minutes.

SAMPLE Which unit is the most appropriate one to use when measuring the weight of several textbooks?

    A ounce   **B** inch   **C** quart   **D** pound

The correct answer is D. Measuring an object's weight requires a unit of weight—ounce or pound. Since textbooks are heavy, you should use the larger of the two units—the pound. Choice A uses a unit that is too small for measuring heavy objects. Choice B is incorrect because an inch is a unit of length. Choice C is incorrect because a quart is a unit of capacity.

1 Which animal's length would be the best to measure in feet?

    A snake   **C** hamster

    B sparrow   **D** spider

2 Alisa needs to measure the capacity of her aquarium. What unit is the best one to use?

    A yard   **C** gallon

    B cup   **D** pound

3 Which is the most appropriate unit to use when measuring how long it takes to sing one verse of "Happy Birthday" to a friend?

    A second   **C** pint

    B mile   **D** minute

4 The Pygmy shrew is one of the smallest mammals on Earth. Which is the best unit to use to weigh this shrew?

    A mile   **C** cup

    B ounce   **D** pound

5 Which of the following would you most likely measure in miles?

    A length of a piece of paper

    B weight of a rock

    C distance between two cities

    D capacity of a bucket

6 Emilio is making a loaf of bread. Which of the following units is he most likely to use to measure the amount of flour he needs?

    A ounce   **C** gallon

    B foot   **D** cup

SAMPLE Would the length of a school bus more likely be 40 feet or 40 miles? Explain your answer.

Answer _____

> The length of a school bus is more likely to be 40 feet. A school bus is large. But its length is not large enough to measure in miles. Miles are used to measure the distance a bus travels. So you should use the smaller of the two units. It is a better choice to use a foot as the unit of measure.

7 During a trip to the vet, Micah's cat was weighed. What unit did the vet most likely use to weigh the cat? Explain your answer.

_____

_____

8 Which lasts more time—a 2-hour movie or a 2-minute commercial? Explain your answer.

_____

_____

9 Roy has a favorite bowl that he uses each morning for cereal. He says that the bowl's capacity should be measured in gallons. His sister says it should be measured in pints. Who is correct? Explain.

_____

_____

_____

10 Ginger and her father are making a new desk for her room. Ginger sketched the plan below to show the measurements of the desktop and the height of the legs. She forgot to write the units.

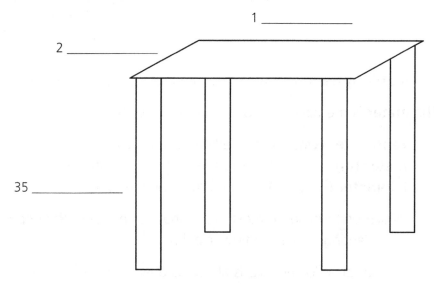

1 _____

2 _____

35 _____

Part A Fill in the blanks in Ginger's plans with the appropriate units of measure for each part of the desk.

Part B When building something like a desk, why is it important to use standard units such as inches and feet? Explain.

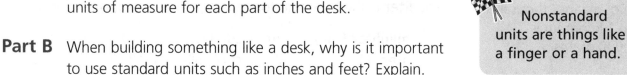

Nonstandard units are things like a finger or a hand.

_____

_____

_____

_____

_____

The metric system is sometimes called the International System (SI). Most countries around the world use the metric system.

In the metric system, prefixes are added to the base units to create larger and smaller units. For example, the prefix *kilo-* means "thousand." So 1 kilogram is 1,000 grams.

Units of length measure how long, wide, tall, or deep something is.

Units of capacity measure how much of something that flows a container holds.

Units of mass measure how heavy something is.

The **metric system** is used to measure length, capacity, and mass.

The **meter** is the base unit for length. Units of **length** include

centimeter (cm)	A housefly is about 1 cm long.
meter (m)	An umbrella is about 1 m in length.
kilometer (km)	A line of 100 elephants is about 1 km long.

Which unit would be most appropriate to measure the depth of a planting hole for a flower bulb?

A hole for a flower bulb is about as deep as your hand is long. So a small unit, centimeters, is the best unit to use.

The **liter** is the base unit for capacity. Units of **capacity** include

milliliter (mL)	An eyedropper can hold about 1 mL.
liter (L)	A quart of milk is a little less than 1 L.

Which unit would be the best to measure the amount of water in a bucket?

The best unit is the one that will give you a measurement with the smallest whole number. You would need a very large number of milliliters to measure the water in a bucket. Use a liter instead.

The **gram** is the base unit for mass. Units of **mass** include

gram (g)	A dollar bill has a mass of about 1 g.
kilogram (kg)	A baseball bat has a mass of about 1 kg.

Which unit would be most appropriate to measure the mass of a cat?

Something with a mass of less than 1 kilogram you could probably hold in one hand. A cat has a mass greater than that, so the kilogram is a better unit to use.

SAMPLE Which of the following would be the most appropriate to measure in centimeters?

    A width of a truck   **C** length of a pencil

    B amount of water in a sink   **D** mass of an apple

> The correct answer is C. A centimeter is a metric unit of length. It is a small unit, so it should be used to measure the length of small objects. Choice A seems correct since you can measure the width of a truck. But a truck is too big to measure using centimeters, so meters are better. Choice B is incorrect because the amount of water in a sink is a measure of capacity, not length. Choice D is incorrect because the mass of an apple does not involve measuring its length.

1 Which is the most appropriate unit to use for measuring the mass of a car?

    A meter   **C** gram

    B kilogram   **D** liter

2 Fatima uses eye drops each morning. Which of the following is the most appropriate unit to use for measuring the amount of eye drops she uses each day?

    A milliliter   **C** gram

    B liter   **D** centimeter

3 Which of the following would be the most appropriate to measure in kilometers?

    A mass of an airplane

    B height of a door

    C amount of water in a lake

    D distance between two cities

4 Jamil needs to buy orange juice to serve 24 people. Which is the most likely amount of orange juice he will buy?

    A 4 mL   **C** 4 L

    B 4 cm   **D** 4 g

5 Which of the following would be the most appropriate to measure in grams?

    A the capacity of a bowl

    B the mass of a spoonful of salt

    C the width of a fingernail

    D the mass of a bag of potatoes

6 When standing on its hind legs, an adult male grizzly bear is taller than an average human. Which of the following units would be the best to use when measuring the height of a grizzly bear?

    A centimeter   **C** kilometer

    B liter   **D** meter

SAMPLE What would you be more likely to measure in liters—the amount of water in a bathtub or the amount of water in a puddle? Explain your answer.

Answer _____

✓ The amount of water in a bathtub is much greater than the amount of water in a puddle. A liter is a larger unit than a milliliter, so you would measure the amount of water in the bathtub in liters.

7 For a science experiment, Malcolm wants to measure the amount of tears produced by a person who cries for 1 minute. He says that the amount of tears will be small so he should use a small metric unit. He decides to measure the amount in centimeters. Explain why Malcolm is incorrect.

_____

_____

_____

8 Would you be more likely to measure the length of an earthworm in centimeters or kilometers? Explain.

_____

_____

_____

9 Kichi says that she needs 2 g of apples to make a pie. Is she correct? Explain.

_____

_____

_____

10 Roger likes to learn the sizes of things to play trivia games. Some of the things he has searched for on the Internet are in the list below.

wingspan of a sparrow: _____

amount of water used to wash dishes: _____

height of a building: _____

mass of a flower: _____

distance traveled by a space shuttle: _____

amount of nail polish in a bottle: _____

mass of a polar bear: _____

Part A For each item on the list, write the most appropriate metric unit to use to measure it.

Part B Which number would be greater—the mass of the polar bear in grams or the mass of the bear in kilograms? Explain.

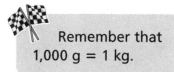

Remember that 1,000 g = 1 kg.

_____

_____

_____

_____

Measurement Conversions

4.MD.1

Metric units are based on 10, so they are easy to multiply or divide by moving the decimal point.

When a larger unit is converted to a smaller unit, the result is a number that is *greater than* the number you started with. When a smaller unit is converted to a larger unit, the result is a number that is *less than* the number you started with.

The different units in each measurement system are related to each other. You can use this information to **convert,** or change between, units of measure to help you compare amounts that use different units.

CUSTOMARY UNITS

Length	Capacity	Weight	Time
1 ft = 12 in.	1 pt = 2 C	1 lb = 16 oz	1 min = 60 sec
1 yd = 36 in.	1 qt = 2 pt		1 hr = 60 min
1 yd = 3 ft	1 gal = 4 qt		
1 mi = 5,280 ft	1 gal = 8 pt		
1 mi = 1,760 yd	1 gal = 16 C		

METRIC UNITS

Length	Capacity	Mass
1 m = 100 cm	1 L = 1,000 mL	1 kg = 1,000 g
1 km = 1,000 m		

To convert from a larger unit to a smaller unit, use multiplication.

A jug holds 4 liters of sweet tea. How many milliliters is this?

To convert liters to milliliters, multiply 4 liters by 1,000, the number of milliliters in 1 liter.

$$4 \text{ L} \times 1,000 = 4,000 \text{ mL}$$

The jug holds 4 liters or 4,000 milliliters of sweet tea.

To convert from a smaller unit to a larger unit, use division.

A coil of rope is 27 feet long. How many yards long is it?

To find the number of yards in 27 feet, divide 27 feet by 3, the number of feet in 1 yard.

$$27 \text{ ft} \div 3 = 9 \text{ yd}$$

The coil of rope is 27 feet or 9 yards long.

You can also use a table to convert units. Write the larger unit in the top row and the smaller unit in the bottom row. Then write the number pairs to show how the units are related.

Yards	1	2	3
Feet	3	6	9

SAMPLE How many centimeters are in 4 meters?

    A 4,000   **B** 400   **C** 40   **D** 4

> The correct answer is B. First find the number of centimeters in
> 1 meter: 1 m = 100 cm. Then multiply to convert from a larger unit
> to a smaller unit: 4 × 100 = 400. So there are 400 centimeters in
> 4 meters.

1 Aldo can hold his breath for about
3 minutes. How many seconds is this?

    A 30   **C** 180

    B 90   **D** 240

2 A bag contains 5 pounds of cat food. How
many ounces is this amount?

    A 50   **C** 80

    B 60   **D** 100

3 The average raccoon has a mass of 4 to
9 kg. The heaviest raccoon found in the
wild had a mass of about 28 kg. What is
the mass of this raccoon in grams?

    A 28 g   **C** 2,800 g

    B 280 g   **D** 28,000 g

4 Sherri is using a cooking pot that can hold
12 quarts. How many gallons can it hold?

    A 3   **C** 6

    B 4   **D** 48

5 Dao bought 3 yards of fabric. How many
inches of fabric did she buy?

    A 108   **C** 12

    B 36   **D** 9

6 Which of the following measurements is
equal to 12,000 mL?

    A 1.2 L   **C** 120 L

    B 12 L   **D** 1,200 L

7 Lynn and Megan live 3.25 km apart. How
many meters is that?

    A 32.5   **C** 3,250

    B 325   **D** 32,500

8 Xavier needs 2 quarts of cream. The store
sells only pints. How many pints must
Xavier buy?

    A 2   **C** 8

    B 4   **D** 16

SAMPLE Manuel's dog weighs 10 pounds. Lianne's dog weighs 192 ounces. Whose dog is heavier? Explain.

Answer _____

Convert one of the units so that you can compare the weights of the dogs in the same units. You can convert pounds to ounces: $10 \times 16 = 160$ oz. Then compare: 160 oz $<$ 192 oz, so Lianne's dog is heavier. Or you can convert ounces to pounds and compare: $192 \div 16 = 12$ lb, and 10 lb $<$ 12 lb, so Lianne's dog is heavier.

9 Eli is seeing a movie that is 2 hours long. Tariq is seeing a movie that is 115 minutes long. Both movies start at the same time. Which movie will end first? Explain how you know.

_____

_____

10 Mina's mother asks her to buy 3,000 grams of oranges. Which bag of oranges should Mina buy? Explain.

 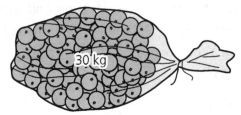

Bag A   Bag B   Bag C

_____

_____

11 Nicole needs to find the number of quarts in 3 gallons. Without converting the units, will the answer be greater than or less than 3? Explain.

_____

_____

12 Noah visited a bird sanctuary with his family. He recorded information he learned about some of the large birds of North America.

LARGE BIRDS OF NORTH AMERICA

Bird	Weight	Wingspan
Canada Goose	12 lb	60 in.
Great Horned Owl	3 lb	50 in.
California Condor	288 oz	3 yd
Turkey Vulture	5 lb	6 ft
American Bald Eagle	208 oz	90 in.

Part A List the birds in order from shortest wingspan to longest wingspan.

_____

_____

_____

_____

_____

> What units are the wingspans given in? What unit will you use to compare them?

Part B Noah wants to compare the birds' weights. He started this table to help him convert pounds to ounces. What mistake did Noah make? Explain.

Pounds	1	2	3	4	5
Ounces	16	32	44	64	80

_____

_____

_____

Measurement Word Problems

4.MD.2

You can use what you know about measurements to solve problems. To solve problems, follow these steps:

1) Read the problem carefully. Identify key information and what you need to find out.
2) Plan how to solve the problem.
3) Solve the problem using your plan.
4) Check your work. Ask yourself if your answer makes sense.

Remember that when a problem involves operations with measurements, the measurements must be in the same units.

Susanna is making 4 quarts of soup. She wants to serve 1 cup of soup per person. Does Susanna have enough soup to serve 20 people?

1. Write down the information you know.
   • Susanna makes 4 qt of soup.
   • Each person will get 1 cup of soup.

2. Tell what the problem is asking you to find, in your own words.
   • Are there 20 1-cup servings, or 20 cups, in 4 quarts?

3. Plan how to find the answer. The measurements are not in the same units. You need to first convert quarts to pints. Then you need to convert pints to cups. Finally, you need to compare the number of cups in 4 quarts to 20 cups.

4. Carry out your plan.
   Convert quarts to pints: 1 qt = 2 pt, so $4 \times 2 = 8$ pt
   Convert pints to cups: 1 pt = 2 C, so $8 \times 2 = 16$ C
   Compare the number of cups to 20: $16 < 20$
   Susanna does not have enough soup to serve 20 people.

5. Check your work, and decide if the answer is reasonable.

   $4 \times 2 \times 2 = 4 \times 4 = 16$ and 16 is less than 20

   Yes, the answer is reasonable.

Solving a word problem can require any operation. Think of key words that are clues to the operations.

Addition—*in all, altogether, total*

Subtraction—*less than, difference, more than*

Multiplication—*total of equal groups, times*

Division—*equal groups, number in each group*

A measurement may be written using a fraction. You can interpret the fraction before or after you do the operation.

One piece of ribbon is $\frac{3}{4}$ meter long. How many centimeters long are 4 pieces this length?

$4 \times \frac{3}{4} = \frac{12}{4} = 3$ m
3×100 cm $= 300$ cm
or
1 m = 100 cm
$4 \times 100 = 400$ cm
$400 \times \frac{3}{4} = 300$ cm

SAMPLE Kai is 5 feet 5 inches tall. His sister is 52 inches tall. What is the difference in their heights?

A 3 inches   **B** 8 inches   **C** 13 inches   **D** 117 inches

The correct answer is C. First, convert Kai's height to inches: 1 foot = 12 inches, so 5 × 12 = 60 inches. Kai is 5 feet 5 inches tall so add the extra 5 inches to 60 inches to find his height: 60 + 5 = 65 inches. You are being asked to find the difference in heights so subtract: 65 − 52 = 13. The difference is 13 inches.

1 One Saturday, Olivia spent 30 minutes cleaning her room, 1 hour raking leaves, and 45 minutes riding her bike. How many minutes in all did Olivia spend doing these activities?

A 135   **C** 76

B 105   **D** 15

2 At a store, apples cost $2.50 per kg. How much will 3 kg of apples cost?

A $2.75   **C** $7.50

B $4.25   **D** $8.00

3 Francisco is making a sub sandwich that will be 2.5 m in length. The sandwich will be divided equally among 10 friends. How many centimeters of the sandwich will each person get?

A 2.5   **C** 250

B 25   **D** 2,500

4 Mr. Nakagawa walked his dog $\frac{3}{10}$ mile and later walked $\frac{7}{10}$ mile on his own. How much farther did he walk on his own than with his dog?

A 1 mile   **C** $\frac{7}{10}$ mile

B $\frac{2}{5}$ mile   **D** $\frac{3}{10}$ mile

5 Tanya drinks $\frac{3}{4}$ L of water a day. How many milliliters of water does she drink in 5 days?

A 5,000   **C** 500

B 3,750   **D** 375

6 A box of 40 DVDs weighs 10 pounds. If all the DVDs are the same weight, how many ounces does each DVD weigh?

A 2   **C** 4

B 3   **D** 5

SAMPLE Liam has $25. A 4-ounce bag of cashews costs $3. Does Liam have enough money to buy 2 pounds of cashews in bags of this size? Explain.

Answer _____

 There are 16 ounces in 1 pound. Multiply to find the ounces in 2 pounds: 2 × 16 = 32 ounces. Divide to find the number of 4-ounces bags: 32 ÷ 4 = 8 bags. Multiply to find the total cost of the bags: 8 × $3 = $24. Compare: $24 < $25. Yes, Liam has enough money.

7 Mrs. Coffey buys the container of spring water here. She uses 4 quarts of water that day. How many quarts of water does Mrs. Coffey have left? Show your work.

2.5 Gallons

Answer _____

8 Geoff made 1.2 kg of trail mix for his hiking club, which has 12 members in all. He wants each hiker to receive the same amount of trail mix. How many grams of trail mix will each hiker get? Show your work.

Answer _____

9 Adita makes dresses for dolls. One style of dress requires $\frac{1}{2}$ foot of ribbon. How many inches of ribbon will Adita need to make 7 of these dresses? Show your work.

Answer _____

10 Marla is conducting an experiment for science class. She grows seedlings and gives them different amounts of sunlight. She records how much the seedlings grow each day.

Part A Marla observed that one seedling grew 1.1 cm on Monday, 1.8 cm on Tuesday, and 1.5 cm on Wednesday. Record the total number of centimeters the seedling grew during the 3 days on the number line below.

> What does each tick mark represent?

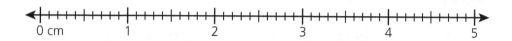

0 cm   1   2   3   4   5

Part B Marla uses 1.8 L of water for the seedlings each week. She uses the same amount of water each day and only waters the seedlings 3 times a week. Marla says that since 1.8 L = 180 mL, she uses 60 mL of water each day she waters the seedlings. Is she correct? Explain.

_____

_____

_____

_____

Measurement Data

4.MD.4

A line plot is sometimes called a **dot plot** and dots are used instead of X's.

A **line plot** uses a number line to display **data,** or information in the form of numbers. Each time a value appears in the data set, an X is placed above that number on the line plot.

Nadia has 6 hamsters. She recorded their weights in the chart below. Make a line plot to display the data.

Weight of Hamsters (in ounces)					
$3\frac{3}{4}$	$3\frac{1}{2}$	$3\frac{1}{4}$	$3\frac{3}{4}$	$3\frac{1}{4}$	$3\frac{1}{8}$

The intervals on a number line should be equal. All the values in this set can be written as equivalent fractions with denominators of 8. So show intervals of $\frac{1}{8}$'s.

Draw a number line. Order the values in the data from least to greatest. Write these on the number line.

$$3\frac{1}{8} \quad 3\frac{1}{4} \quad 3\frac{3}{8} \quad 3\frac{1}{2} \quad 3\frac{5}{8} \quad 3\frac{3}{4}$$

If the same value appears more than once in the data, only list the value once on the number line.

Place an X above each value in the line plot to show how many times it appears in the data. For example, $3\frac{1}{4}$ appears twice. So place two X's above $3\frac{1}{4}$ in the line plot.

$$3\frac{1}{8} \quad 3\frac{1}{4} \quad 3\frac{3}{8} \quad 3\frac{1}{2} \quad 3\frac{5}{8} \quad 3\frac{3}{4}$$

You can use a line plot to solve measurement problems.

You can only add or subtract fractions with **like denominators.** Change $3\frac{3}{4}$ to $3\frac{6}{8}$ by multiplying the numerator and denominator by 2.

What is the difference in weight between the heaviest and lightest hamsters?

Find the information in the line plot. The heaviest hamster is $3\frac{3}{4}$ oz. The lightest hamster is $3\frac{1}{8}$ oz. To find the difference, you need to subtract.

$$3\frac{3}{4} - 3\frac{1}{8} = 3\frac{6}{8} - 3\frac{1}{8} = \frac{5}{8}$$

The difference is $\frac{5}{8}$ oz.

SAMPLE Connor measured the lengths of 8 Gypsy moth caterpillars he found in his backyard. He recorded the data here.

Lengths of Caterpillars (cm)
$4\frac{1}{3}$ $4\frac{2}{3}$ $4\frac{1}{2}$ $4\frac{1}{6}$ $4\frac{1}{3}$ $4\frac{5}{6}$ $4\frac{1}{2}$ $4\frac{1}{3}$

How many X's should be used for the value of $4\frac{1}{2}$ in a line plot for this data?

A 2 　　　 **B** 3 　　　 **C** 4 　　　 **D** 5

The correct answer is A. The value for $4\frac{1}{2}$ appears 2 times in the data. So you would write 2 X's for this value. The other answer choices are incorrect because $4\frac{1}{2}$ does not appear more than twice.

Use the line plot below to answer questions 1 and 2.

NOLA'S RIBBONS

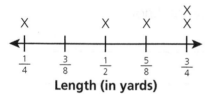

Length (in yards)

1 How many ribbons does Nola have?

A 3 　　　　　 **C** 5

B 4 　　　　　 **D** 6

2 What is the difference in length between the longest and shortest ribbons?

A $\frac{1}{4}$ yd 　　　 **C** $\frac{5}{8}$ yd

B $\frac{1}{2}$ yd 　　　 **D** $\frac{3}{4}$ yd

Use the line plot below to answer questions 3 and 4.

HEIGHTS OF STUDENTS

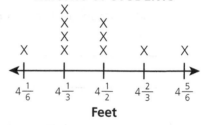

Feet

3 What is the difference in height between the tallest and shortest students?

A $\frac{2}{3}$ ft 　　　 **C** $\frac{1}{2}$ ft

B $4\frac{1}{6}$ ft 　　　 **D** $4\frac{5}{6}$ ft

4 How many students are $4\frac{1}{3}$ feet tall?

A 1 　　　　　 **C** 3

B 2 　　　　　 **D** 4

SAMPLE Donna made this line plot to show the lengths of the windows in her house.

How many windows are more than $1\frac{1}{5}$ meters tall?

WINDOW LENGTHS

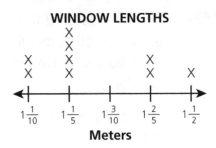

Meters

Answer _____

 In a line plot, each X stands for 1 data value. So count the number of X's above lengths that are greater than $1\frac{1}{5}$ meters. Lengths greater than $1\frac{1}{5}$ appear to the right of that number on the number line. There are 2 X's above $1\frac{2}{5}$ and 1 X above $1\frac{1}{2}$. So there are 3 windows that are taller than $1\frac{1}{5}$ meters.

Use the line plot above to answer questions 5 and 6.

5 Are the intervals shown on the line plot equal? Explain how you know.

_____

_____

6 How much taller is the tallest window than the shortest window?

Answer _____

7 Olaf recorded the number of minutes it took for six friends to run a mile.

$$9\frac{1}{2} \quad 9\frac{1}{4} \quad 9\frac{7}{8} \quad 9\frac{1}{2} \quad 9\frac{1}{8} \quad 9\frac{1}{4}$$

Make a line plot for the data in the space below.

8 Keith and Derek are testing a new recipe for fruit punch. The ingredients are listed below.

Fruit Punch

$\frac{1}{4}$ L pineapple juice $\frac{1}{2}$ L apple juice

$\frac{1}{2}$ L cranberry juice $\frac{1}{4}$ L pomegranate juice

$\frac{3}{4}$ L orange juice $\frac{1}{4}$ L ginger ale

Part A Make a line plot to display the juice data from the recipe.

Part B How many liters of fruit punch will this recipe make?

Answer _____

To add or subtract fractions, the denominators of both fractions must be the same. Write equivalent fractions so that the fractions have like denominators.

REVIEW

Measurement

Read each problem. Circle the letter of the best answer.

1 Which of the following would be the most appropriate to measure in gallons?

A   width of a human hair

B   weight of a backpack

C   amount of water in a barrel

D   height of a flagpole

2 How many kilograms are equal to 7,000 grams?

A   7

B   70

C   700

D   70,000

3 Look at this line plot.

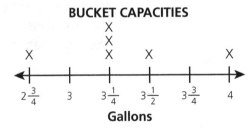

BUCKET CAPACITIES

Gallons

What is the difference in capacity between the largest and smallest buckets?

A $\frac{1}{4}$ gal

B $1\frac{1}{4}$ gal

C   2 gal

D $13\frac{1}{2}$ gal

4 Lucas wants to measure the amount of water in a barrel. Which unit is the most appropriate one to use?

A   gram

B   milliliter

C   liter

D   kilometer

5 A bag of dog food with a mass of 2.5 kg costs $2.50. How much will 3 bags cost?

A $1.75

B $2.50

C $5.25

D $7.50

6 Which of the following is the most appropriate unit to use to measure the length of an envelope?

A   m

B   mL

C   cm

D   km

7 When a tree was planted, it stood 37 inches tall. Ten years later, the tree was 8 feet tall. How many inches did the tree grow?

A   9

B   29

C   59

D   69

8 Is the weight of a moth more likely to be 3 ounces or 3 pounds?
Explain.

_____

_____

9 Pilar ran 2 km and her brother ran 200 m. She says that they ran the
same distance. Is she correct? Explain.

_____

_____

10 Mrs. Kim is rewiring the 4 speakers in her living room. She needs
$1\frac{1}{2}$ feet of wire for each speaker. How many inches of wire does she
need to buy? Show your work.

Answer _____

11 Dan wants to listen to an audio book that runs for 144 minutes. He is
taking a plane trip that lasts 2 hours 30 minutes. Can Dan listen to the
entire audio book? Explain.

_____

_____

_____

12 Rihana is planning a garden. She picks some kinds of flowers and
records the average height of each type on this line plot.

How many kinds of flowers are at least $1\frac{1}{2}$ feet tall?

Answer _____

HEIGHTS OF FLOWERS

```
          X     X
    X     X     X     X
    X     X     X     X
  ←─┼─────┼─────┼─────┼─→
   1 1/6  1 1/3  1 1/2  1 2/3
          Feet
```

13 Akira is painting the ceilings in hotel rooms. He uses 3 pints of paint to paint each ceiling.

Part A How many quarts of paint does Akira need for 12 ceilings? Show your work.

Answer _____

Part B At the paint store, Akira sees that 1 gallon of paint costs $15.97. There is also a sale on quart-sized cans of paint. Each quart costs $3.50. Should Akira buy the gallon cans or the quart cans? Explain.

_____

_____

_____

14 Ravi visited a chicken farm and helped weigh some eggs. He recorded the number of ounces each egg weighed.

$1\frac{2}{3}$	$1\frac{1}{3}$	$1\frac{1}{2}$	$1\frac{1}{6}$	$1\frac{2}{3}$	$1\frac{1}{2}$	$1\frac{1}{3}$	$1\frac{1}{2}$	$1\frac{2}{3}$

Part A Draw a line plot for the data.

Part B What is the difference in weight between the heaviest egg and the lightest egg?

Answer _____

Perimeter and Area

- **Lesson 1 Perimeter of Rectangles** reviews how to use a formula to find the perimeter of a rectangle.

- **Lesson 2 Area of Rectangles** reviews how to use a formula to find the area of a rectangle.

Perimeter of Rectangles

4.MD.3

 Perimeter is a measure of length, so it is written using units of length, such as feet or meters.

Perimeter is the distance around a figure. You can find the perimeter of any figure by adding the lengths of the sides.

Find the perimeter of this rectangle.

$l = 6$ cm

$w = 4$ cm

A rectangle has four sides, and the opposite sides are the same lengths. The lengths of the sides of this rectangle are 4 cm, 6 cm, 4 cm, and 6 cm. Add to find perimeter.

$$6 + 4 + 6 + 4 = 20 \text{ cm}$$

You can also find the perimeter of a rectangle by using a formula.

A **formula** is an equation that states a rule. The rule is always true for the values put in it.

Perimeter formula:
$P = (2 \times l) + (2 \times w)$
l = length
w = width
P = perimeter

Rose puts a fence around a rectangular vegetable garden. The garden is 12 meters long and 8 meters wide. How long is the fence?

Use the perimeter formula.

A rectangle has 2 sides of the same length: 2 × length
It has 2 sides of the same width: 2 × width

Add the products together to find the sum:

Perimeter = (2 × length) + (2 × width)

Use the given values for the length and width in the formula: length = 12 and width = 8

Multiply: $P = (2 \times 12) + (2 \times 8)$
Add: $P = (24) + (16)$
       $P = 40$

Rose put a 40-meter fence around the garden.

Read each problem. Circle the letter of the best answer.

SAMPLE What is the perimeter of this rectangle?

A 8 m   C 16 m

B 15 m   D 34 m

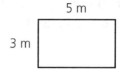

5 m

3 m

The correct answer is C. The perimeter is the distance around a figure. So it is the sum of the lengths of the sides. Since the opposite sides of a rectangle are the same length, you can multiply each length by 2 and add the sum: (2 × 5) + (2 × 3) = 10 + 6 = 16. The perimeter is 16 meters.

1 Leila designed this card. What is the perimeter of the card?

14 cm

Happy Birthday!

9 cm

A 23 cm   C 126 cm

B 46 cm   D 277 cm

2 Hal's room is a rectangle. It is 18 ft long and 13 ft wide. What is the room's perimeter?

A 18 ft   C 36 ft

B 31 ft   D 62 ft

3 Which is the formula for the perimeter of a rectangle?

A $P = (l \times w)$

B $P = 2(l \times w)$

C $P = (2 \times l) + (2 \times w)$

D $P = (2 + l) \times (2 + w)$

4 Each square on the grid has a side length of 1 in. Which is the perimeter of the shaded rectangle?

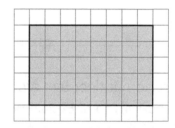

A 13 in.   C 32 in.

B 26 in.   D 64 in.

5 Which statement about these rectangles is true?

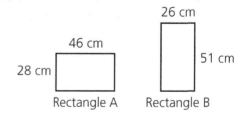

26 cm

46 cm

51 cm

28 cm

Rectangle A   Rectangle B

A The perimeters cannot be compared.

B The perimeters are the same.

C Rectangle A's perimeter is greater.

D Rectangle B's perimeter is greater.

SAMPLE A rectangle is 22 feet long and 13 feet wide. Another rectangle has the same perimeter, but it is 15 feet wide. How long is the second rectangle?

Answer _____

✓   Use the formula to find the perimeter of the first rectangle: $P = (2 \times 22) + (2 \times 13) = 44 + 26 = 70$ feet. The second rectangle has the same perimeter, 70 feet, but different dimensions. Subtract the known width: $70 - (2 \times 15) = 70 - 30 = 40$. This means that $2 \times \text{length} = 40$. Divide by 2: $40 \div 2 = 20$. So the second rectangle is 20 feet long.

6 A rectangular message board is 31 inches long and 21 inches wide. What is the perimeter of the board? Show your work.

Answer _____

7 Trina plans to put floor trim around the perimeter of her den. The den is a rectangular room. Explain why Trina does **not** need to measure all four sides of the room to find the perimeter.

_____

_____

8 Boyd's backyard is a rectangle. It is 39 m long and 11 m wide. Boyd says the perimeter of the backyard is 50 m. What is Boyd's mistake? What is the perimeter of the backyard?

_____

_____

_____

9 Sylvia knows that a rectangle is 8 yards wide. The length is twice the width. How can Sylvia find the perimeter? Explain.

_____

_____

10 Pete and Tilda jog every afternoon. Pete jogs around park A with a length of 67 m and a width of 33 m. Tilda jogs around park B. Half the length of park B is 41 m and it width is 27 m.

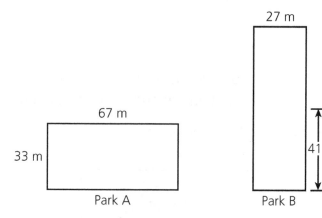

Part A What is the perimeter of each park? Show your work.

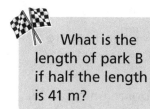

What is the length of park B if half the length is 41 m?

Park A _____

Park B _____

Part B Pete says the perimeter of park A is 200 m and the perimeter of park B is 136 m. He believes he jogs more meters than Tilda. What is Pete's mistake? Explain.

_____

_____

_____

_____

Area of Rectangles

4.MD.3

Area is the amount of space inside a plane figure. You can measure the area of a rectangle by counting the number of square units inside it.

What is the area of this rectangle?

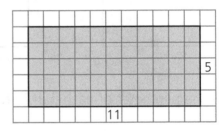

You can count the square units inside the rectangle. You can count the squares in one row and multiply by the number of rows.

There are 11 squares in each row. There are 5 rows.

11 squares × 5 rows = 55 square units

You can also find the area of a rectangle by using a formula.

Len plants grass seed in his backyard. His backyard is a rectangle 25 meters long and 14 meters wide. What is the area of the rectangle Len plants with grass seed?

Use the area formula.

Area = length × width

Find the **dimensions,** or length and width, of the rectangle: length = 25 m and width = 14 m. Use them in the formula.

Multiply: $A = 25 × 14$

$A = 350$ square meters

Len plants an area of 350 square meters, or 350 m².

Area is measured in square units. A **square unit** is 1 unit long and 1 unit wide.

☐ = 1 square unit
$1 × 1 = 1^2$

Square units can be square meters (m²), square centimeters (cm²), square feet (ft²), and square inches (in.²).

The area formula is the same as multiplying the number of squares in a row by the number of rows.

Area = length × width

$A = lw$

SAMPLE Oliver prints out a photo on his computer, as shown here. The size of the photo is 13 cm by 17 cm. What is the area of the photo?

13 cm

17 cm

A 30 cm²

C 221 cm²

B 60 cm²

D 266 cm²

The correct answer is C. The diagram shows a photo that is a rectangle, so use the rectangle formula to find the area: $A = l \times w$. Multiply the length and the width: $17 \times 13 = 221$ square cm, or cm². The photo has an area of 221 cm².

1 Each square on the grid is 1 in. What is the area of the shaded rectangle?

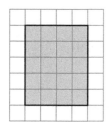

A 9 in.²

C 25 in.²

B 20 in.²

D 40 in.²

2 A hotel meeting room is a rectangle 32 m long and 25 m wide. What is the area?

A 57 m²

C 228 m²

B 114 m²

D 800 m²

3 The length of a rectangle is 38 ft and the width is 11 ft. What is the area?

A 29 ft²

C 418 ft²

B 58 ft²

D 836 ft²

4 Robin wants to find the area of a rectangle. Which formula should she use?

A $A = l \times w$

B $A = 2(l \times w)$

C $A = (2 \times l) + (2 \times w)$

D $A = (2 + l) \times (2 + w)$

5 Which statement about these rectangles is true?

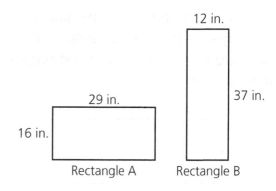

12 in.

29 in.

37 in.

16 in.

Rectangle A   Rectangle B

A Rectangle A has a larger area.

B Rectangle B has a larger area.

C The rectangles have the same area.

D The areas cannot be compared.

SAMPLE The length of a rectangle is 44 cm and the width is 22 cm. Truman says the area of this rectangle is 66 square cm. Is Truman correct? Explain.

Answer _____

✓ The number 66 is the sum of 44 and 22, so Truman is not correct. To find the area of the rectangle, find the product of 44 and 22. Multiply the length by the width: 44 × 22 = 968. The area is 968 cm².

6 The length of a rectangle is 45 m long and the width is 23 m long. What is the area of the rectangle? Show your work.

Answer _____

7 The area of a horse's stall is 108 square feet. Lana knows that the stall is 9 feet wide. How could Lana use the area formula to find the length of the stall?

_____

_____

_____

8 Look at the rectangles on the grid. Which rectangle has the greatest area? Explain how you found your answer and support it with proof.

_____

_____

_____

_____

_____

_____

9 Carla's bedroom is a rectangle with length 15 feet and width 8 feet. She wants to put a carpet in the room.

Part A Draw a rectangle to represent Carla's bedroom on the grid below. Label it with the length and width. Then use the area formula to find the area of the room. Show your work.

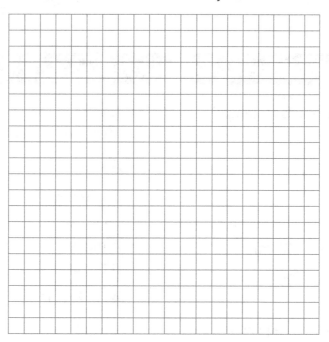

Answer _____

Part B Carpet A is 13 feet long and 9 feet wide. Carpet B is 16 feet long and 7 feet wide. Carla thinks the area of the room is greater than the area of each carpet, so either carpet will fit. Draw each carpet on the room on the grid. What is Carla's mistake? Explain your answer.

How does each dimension of the carpets compare to the length and width of the room?

_____

_____

_____

_____

_____

REVIEW

Perimeter and Area

Read each problem. Circle the letter of the best answer.

1 What is the perimeter of this rectangle?

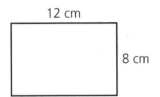

12 cm

8 cm

A 20 cm   **C** 40 cm

B 30 cm   **D** 96 cm

2 Each square on the grid is 1 square in. What is the area of the shaded rectangle?

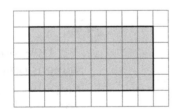

A 12 in.^{2} **C** 32 in.^{2}

B 24 in.^{2} **D** 64 in.^{2}

3 A rectangle is 29 feet long and 11 feet wide. What is the perimeter of the rectangle?

A 40 ft   **C** 160 ft

B 80 ft   **D** 320 ft

4 A rectangular parking lot is 40 m long and 30 m wide. What is its area?

A 70 m^2 **C** 1,200 m^2

B 140 m^2 **D** 1,400 m^2

5 A rug is 9 feet long and 8 feet wide. What is the area of the rug?

A 17 feet^2 **C** 68 feet^2

B 34 feet^2 **D** 72 feet^2

6 Which statement about the rectangles is true?

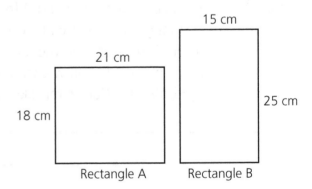

15 cm

21 cm

18 cm

25 cm

Rectangle A   Rectangle B

A Rectangle A's perimeter is greater.

B Rectangle B's perimeter is greater.

C They have the same perimeter.

D The perimeters cannot be compared.

7 The length of a rectangle is 50 inches and the width is 10 inches. Explain how to find the perimeter of the rectangle. Then find the perimeter.

_____

_____

8 A fence marks the perimeter of a rectangular field. The field is 34 meters long and 14 meters wide. Kevin says the fence must be 48 meters in length. What mistake did he make? What is the correct perimeter?

_____

_____

9 The length of a rectangle is 62 cm and the width is 14 cm. What is the area of the rectangle? Show your work.

Answer _____

10 On the grid, draw a rectangle that has an area of 24 square units.

Use the area formula to prove your rectangle has this area.

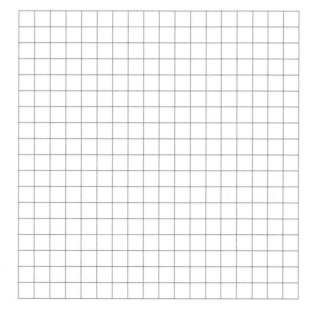

Answer _____

11 Erin is painting flats for a school play. A flat is a rectangular panel that the background is painted on.

Part A Erin paints the wall of a house on a flat that is 8 feet long and 6 feet high. What is the area of the flat? Use the area formula and show your work.

Answer _____

Part B Erin needs to cut out a rectangle from the flat for a window. The window will be 2 feet wide and 3 feet long. Draw the flat and the window on the grid below.

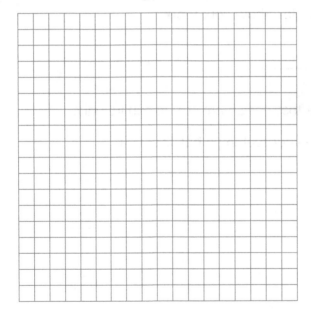

What will be the area of the flat after the window is cut out? Explain how you found your answer.

_____

_____

_____

_____

Geometry

● **Lesson 1 Points, Lines, Rays, and Angles** reviews how to identify common plane figures in geometry.

● **Lesson 2 Angle Measure** reviews how to measure angles, classify angles by their measures, and add and subtract angle measures to solve problems.

● **Lesson 3 Parallel and Perpendicular Lines** reviews parallel and perpendicular lines and their characteristics.

● **Lesson 4 Classifying Shapes** reviews how to identify types of triangles and quadrilaterals.

● **Lesson 5 Lines of Symmetry** reviews how to draw lines of symmetry and identify shapes that have lines of symmetry.

UNIT 9
Geometry
163

© The Continental Press, Inc.   DUPLICATING THIS MATERIAL IS ILLEGAL.

Points, Lines, Rays, and Angles

4.G.1

A point is marked with a small dot.

You can identify a line because there are arrows at both ends of the figure.

Use symbols to name these figures:

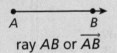

A   B
line AB or $\overleftrightarrow{AB}$

A   B
line segment AB or $\overline{AB}$

A   B
ray AB or $\overrightarrow{AB}$

You can name an angle in different ways.

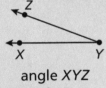

angle XYZ
angle ZYX
angle Y

You can also use the symbol ∠ to name an angle:

∠XYZ
∠ZYX
∠Y

Points, lines, rays, and angles are common geometric figures.

Look at the figure below.

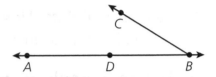

What are the names of the points on this figure?

A **point** is a fixed location in space. The letters A, B, C, and D name points in this figure.

What is the name of the line on this figure?

A **line** is a figure made up of points that extends forever in both directions. It is named for two points on it. Line AB is in this figure.

What is the name of a line segment on this figure?

A **line segment** is a piece of a line. Its ends are marked by **endpoints.** Use the endpoints to name the line segment. This figure includes line segments AD, AB, DB, and BC.

What is the name of a ray on this figure?

A **ray** has one endpoint and continues forever in the other direction. This figure includes rays BC, BA, and DA.

If two rays share an endpoint and extend in different directions, they form an **angle.**

What is the name of an angle on the figure above?

Point B is shared by ray BC and ray BA. These rays form angle ABC, or ∠ABC.

SAMPLE What type of geometric figure is shown here?

M   N

    A point   **B** line   **C** ray   **D** line segment

The correct answer is D. A line segment is part of a line, or a set of points, with two endpoints that define its length. In this figure, points *M* and *N* are the endpoints for the line segment.

---

1 An angle has a vertex at point *K* with point *J* on one ray and point *L* on the other. Which of the following could **not** be used to name this angle?

  A angle *K*   **C** angle *LKJ*

  B angle *JKL*   **D** angle *JLK*

2 Paco drew a figure by connecting points along a line. He drew arrows at each end. He identified two points on his figure as *P* and *Q*. Which of the following can be used to name Paco's figure?

  A $\overleftrightarrow{PQ}$ **C** $\overline{PQ}$

  B $\overrightarrow{PQ}$ **D** ∠*PQ*

3 Which geometric figure extends forever in only one direction?

  A line   **C** line segment

  B ray   **D** angle

4 Kay drew angle *MNP*. Which of the following shows angle *MNP*?

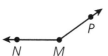

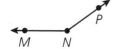
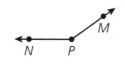

5 Which of the following names an endpoint on this figure?

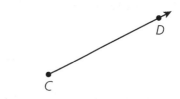

  A *XY*   **C** *Y*

  B *Z*   **D** *X*

6 Walter put his math book on his desk and opened it halfway. If the sides of the book extended forever, what kind of figure would Walter have formed with his book?

  A line segment   **C** line

  B angle   **D** ray

7 Which of the following names the figure shown below?

C   D

  A $\overleftrightarrow{CD}$ **C** ∠*CD*

  B $\overrightarrow{CD}$ **D** $\overline{CD}$

SAMPLE Tim drew the figure pictured at the right. List and name the points, line segments, rays, and angle in Tim's drawing.

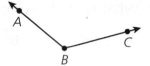

Points _____   Rays _____

Line segments _____   Angle _____

 Points name a specific location in space. This figure includes points *A*, *B*, and *C*. Line segments are part of a line. They have two endpoints. There are two line segments in this figure: $\overline{AB}$ and $\overline{BC}$. Rays have one endpoint. A ray extends forever in the other direction. There are two rays: $\overrightarrow{BA}$ and $\overrightarrow{BC}$. An angle is made up of two rays. Rays *BA* and *BC* form angle *ABC* in this figure.

8 Jun drew ray *PS*. Then she drew ray *PT*. Both rays share the same endpoint *P*. What is another name for point *P*?

Answer _____

9 Draw and name the geometric figure formed by $\overrightarrow{UV}$ and $\overrightarrow{UW}$.

Answer _____

10 Lacey drew a geometric figure that had endpoints *Q* and *R*. Draw Lacey's figure in the space at the right. Name the figure.

Answer _____

11 Patrick drew the geometric figure below.

He named the figure ray *GF*. Explain why this name is incorrect.

_____

_____

12 Geometric figures can contain points, lines, line segments, rays, and angles.

Part A In the space below, draw line *BC*. Draw point *A* on line *BC*. Draw ray *AD*.

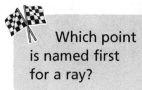

Which point is named first for a ray?

Part B Name all the geometric figures formed.

Points _____

Lines _____

Line segments _____

Rays _____

Angles _____

Angle Measure

4.MD.5.a, b; 4.MD.6; 4.MD.7

The measure of an angle is found in **degrees.** The symbol ° means "degrees."

90° means "90 degrees"

The ∠ symbol means "angle." An m in front of the ∠ means "the measure of an angle."

m∠Y means "measure of angle Y"

An angle is measured as part of a circle. If the vertex is at the center of the circle, the angle's measure is a fraction of the circle.

Angle X is a right angle. It measures 90°, or $\frac{1}{4}$ of the circle.

A circle measures 360°.

A protractor shows two sets of numbers. Be sure to read each set from the correct direction.

Angles can be classified by their measures.

Acute   **Right**   **Obtuse**   **Straight**

What types of angles are in the figure below?

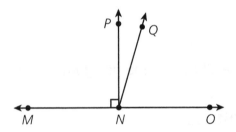

Angles *ONQ* and *PNQ* are **acute** angles. They are smaller than 90°.

Angles *PNM* and *PNO* are **right** angles. They are exactly 90°.

Angle *MNQ* is an **obtuse** angle. It is greater than 90° but less than 180°.

Angle *MNO* is a **straight** angle. It is exactly 180°.

You measure an angle using a tool called a **protractor.**

What is the measure of ∠R?

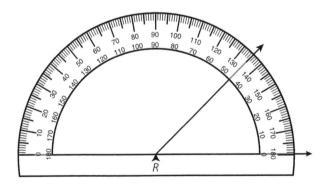

To measure an angle using a protractor, line up 0° with one ray of the angle. Find the point along the protractor where the angle's other ray lines up. Read the measure. Angle *R* measures 45°.

SAMPLE Angle *QRS* has a measure of 128° and angle *QRP* has a measure of 63°. What is the measure of angle *PRS?*

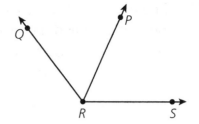

A   65°   C   191°

B   128°   D   193°

The correct answer is A. To find the measure of angle *PRS,* subtract the measure of angle *QRP* from the measure of angle *QRS:* 128° − 63° = 65°.

1 Maya's teacher asked her to draw a 25° angle. Which angle did Maya draw?

A   C

B   D

2 What is the measure of the angle below? Use your protractor.

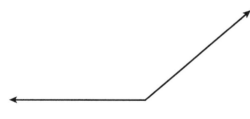

A   40°   C   130°

B   50°   D   140°

3 Yvette drew an angle that had a measure of 100°. What kind of angle did Yvette draw?

A   acute   C   right

B   obtuse   D   straight

4 Lon drew two angles. The measure of the first angle was 165°. The sum of the measures of the angles was 180°. What was the measure of the second angle?

A   15°   C   90°

B   75°   D   180°

5 In the figure below, ∠*ABD* measures 110°.

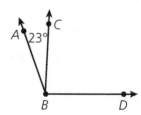

Which number sentence could you use to find m∠*CBD?*

A   m∠*CBD* + 110° = 23°

B   m∠*CBD* − 23° = 110°

C   m∠*CBD* + 23° = 110°

D   180° − m∠*CBD* = 23°

SAMPLE The map shows a section of Turnersville. Use a
protractor to find the measure of angle *A* at
the corner of Broadway and Washington Street.

Answer _____

To find the measure of angle *A*, line up
the 0 on the protractor with Broadway.
Then find the mark on the protractor where
Washington Street lines up. This is at 70°.

6 Orlando measures angle *B* at the corner of Madison Street and
Broadway and finds that it is a 110° angle. What is the measure of
angle *C*? Explain how you found your answer.

_____

_____

_____

7 Use your protractor to help you answer this question.

Angles *MNO* and *PNO* share ray *NO*. Angle *MNO*
measures 35°. Angle *PNO* measures 40°. Draw these
angles in the space at the right. What is the measure
of angle *MNP*?

Answer _____

8 Use your protractor to help you answer this question.

Angle *FGH* measures 90°. In the space at the right, draw
and label angle *FGH*. What kind of angle is angle *FGH*?

Answer _____

UNIT 9 ▨▨▨▨▨▨▨▨▨▨▨▨▨▨▨▨▨▨▨▨▨▨▨▨▨▨▨▨▨▨
Geometry

9 Hana is baking bread. She is using a kitchen timer that has a circle for a dial. One hand of the timer points to 0. The other hand moves to mark the amount of time. She sets the dial for 25 minutes, as shown below.

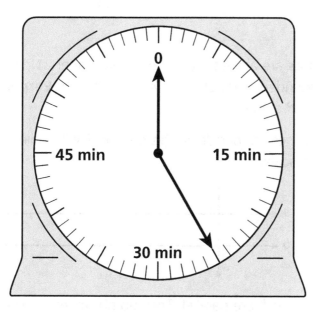

Part A Use a protractor to find the measure of the angle the timer is set to.

Answer _____

Part B After 5 minutes, Hana checks on the bread. The hand that measures time has moved 30° closer to 0. What is the measure of the angle formed by the hand at 0 and the hand that tells how much time is left? Explain how you found your answer.

Imagine drawing another ray to show the angle of the timer after 5 minutes has passed. How is this angle related to the original angle?

_____

_____

_____

_____

Parallel and Perpendicular Lines

4.G.1

LESSON 3

Parallel lines are always the same distance apart. No matter how far they are extended, parallel lines will never touch. **Perpendicular lines** meet at a 90° angle.

Which lines are parallel in this diagram? Which lines are perpendicular?

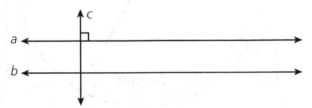

Lines *a* and *b* are parallel. They do not meet. They are always the same distance apart.

Lines *a* and *c* are perpendicular. They meet to form a 90° angle. This angle is marked by a small square. Lines *b* and *c* are also perpendicular.

Many polygons have parallel and perpendicular sides.

Which two sides of this trapezoid are parallel? Which sides are perpendicular?

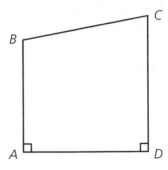

Sides *AB* and *DC* are parallel. They do not meet. They stay the same distance apart. If you extended these sides forever, they would never meet.

Sides *AB* and *AD* are perpendicular. So are sides *DC* and *AD*. These sets of sides meet at right angles.

Line segments and rays can also be parallel and perpendicular.

These line segments are perpendicular.

These rays are parallel.

A small square in an angle shows that it is a right angle.

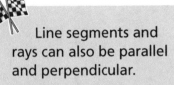

SAMPLE In the diagram here, which lines are parallel?

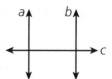

A   lines *a* and *c*   C   lines *a* and *b*

B   lines *b* and *c*   D   lines *a*, *b*, and *c*

 The correct answer is C. Lines *a* and *b* are always the same distance apart and never touch. So they are parallel lines.

1 Which sides in the figure below are perpendicular?

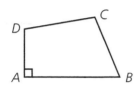

A $\overline{AB}$ and $\overline{BC}$ C $\overline{DA}$ and $\overline{AB}$

B $\overline{BC}$ and $\overline{CD}$ D $\overline{AB}$ and $\overline{CD}$

2 Alicia has four charms for her charm bracelet. Which charm has a pair of parallel sides?

A

B

C

D

3 Briana drew a shape with four sides that were all perpendicular to the adjacent sides. What shape could Briana have drawn?

A   trapezoid   C   parallelogram

B   square   D   right triangle

4 Carter used a computer drawing program to draw a pair of parallel lines. Then he turned one of the lines 90°. What word describes the lines now?

A   perpendicular   C   even

B   parallel   D   square

5 Which of the following shows a pair of parallel line segments?

A   C

B   D

6 Two parallel lines *a* and *b* are perpendicular to line *c*. Line *c* is parallel to line *d*. Which is **not** true about line *d*?

A   Line *d* is parallel to line *a*.

B   Line *d* is perpendicular to line *b*.

C   Line *d* is parallel to line *c*.

D   Line *d* is perpendicular to line *a*.

UNIT 9
Geometry

173

SAMPLE Look at the figure at the right.

What are two line segments that are perpendicular in this figure?

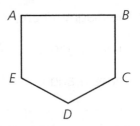

Answer _____

Perpendicular line segments meet at a right angle. Look for line segments that form a right angle, or a square corner. In this figure, there are two sets of perpendicular line segments. Line segments *AE* and *AB* are perpendicular. Line segments *AB* and *BC* are also perpendicular.

7 In the space below, draw $\overrightarrow{MN}$ parallel to $\overrightarrow{OP}$.

8 Christopher drew lines *f* and *g* so that they are parallel. He wants to draw line *h* so it is perpendicular to line *f* but not to line *g*. Explain why this is not possible.

_____

_____

_____

_____

9 In the space below, draw $\overleftrightarrow{PQ}$ parallel to $\overleftrightarrow{RS}$. Then draw $\overrightarrow{ST}$ perpendicular to $\overleftrightarrow{RS}$.

10 Mrs. Arimoto gave these instructions to her class.

1. Draw two parallel lines. Label the lines *x* and *y*.

2. Draw a line that is perpendicular to the lines. Label the line *z*.

Part A Use the space below to draw the figure Mrs. Arimoto's students drew.

Part B What type of angles are formed by these lines? Explain how you know.

_____

_____

_____

_____

_____

What is the measure of each angle? What kind of angle has this measure?

Classifying Shapes

4.G.2

A **polygon** is a two-dimensional figure with line segments for sides.

Perpendicular lines form right angles.

Parallel lines are always the same distance apart.

A **square** is a rectangle with all sides the same length.

A **rhombus** is a parallelogram with all sides the same length.

A rectangle is also a parallelogram because it has opposite sides that are parallel. Not every parallelogram is a rectangle.

All squares are rectangles and rhombuses. But not all rectangles or rhombuses are squares.

Triangles are polygons with three sides. They can be classified by their angles.

  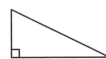

An **acute triangle** has three acute angles.

An **obtuse triangle** has one obtuse angle.

A **right triangle** has one right angle.

A triangle has one angle that measures 135°. The other two angles measure 20° and 25°. What type of triangle is it?

An angle that measures 135° is an obtuse angle. The other two angles are acute. A triangle with one obtuse angle is an obtuse triangle.

Quadrilaterals are polygons with four sides. They can be classified by their angles or the lines that form their sides.

A **parallelogram** has opposite sides that are parallel.

A **rectangle** has four right angles. It has opposite sides that are parallel.

A **trapezoid** has only one pair of parallel sides.

What type of figure is shown below?

This polygon has four sides. Only one pair of the sides is parallel. The other pair is not parallel. They are not always the same distance apart. This is a trapezoid.

SAMPLE Which type of figure is shown below?

- **A** rectangle
- **C** obtuse triangle
- **B** parallelogram
- **D** trapezoid

The correct answer is B. The figure has four sides, so it is a quadrilateral, not a triangle. The opposite sides are parallel, but the angles are not right angles. This figure is a parallelogram.

1 Which of these figures is an acute triangle?

A

C

B

D

2 Parker drew a polygon with four sides. It had one pair of parallel sides. The other pair of sides was not parallel. What type of polygon did Parker draw?

- **A** rhombus
- **C** square
- **B** rectangle
- **D** trapezoid

3 Which of these figures always has a 90° angle?

- **A** trapezoid
- **C** right triangle
- **B** rhombus
- **D** acute triangle

4 A certain polygon has three sides. It has three angles. One angle measures 108°. What is this polygon?

- **A** right triangle
- **C** acute triangle
- **B** obtuse triangle
- **D** parallelogram

5 Stewart's teacher asks him to draw a quadrilateral with four right angles that is not a square. What type of figure should Stewart draw?

- **A** rectangle
- **C** trapezoid
- **B** right triangle
- **D** rhombus

6 Which of the following figures is **not** a parallelogram?

A   **C**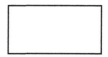

B   **D**

SAMPLE A yield sign is in the shape of a triangle. Based on its angles, what type of triangle is this sign?

Answer _____

    All of the angles in the triangle are acute. This means they are less than 90°. So the sign is an acute triangle.

7 In the space at the right, draw a rhombus that is not a square.

8 Jayson drew a rectangle. Then he drew a diagonal line from one corner to the opposite corner. He ended up with two congruent triangles. How can these triangles be classified by their angles?

_____

_____

9 Nina says that a square can also be a trapezoid. Is she correct? Explain.

_____

_____

_____

10 Juan wrote down the following statements after learning how to classify quadrilaterals. Is he correct? Explain.

All squares are rhombuses.
All squares are rectangles.
So all rhombuses are rectangles.

_____

_____

_____

_____

11 Samir made this painting using different geometric figures.

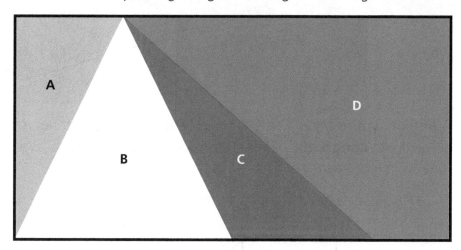

Part A Name the shape of the entire painting. Name the shapes of the figures in the painting.

> Look at each figure in the painting. Count the number of sides. Look at the sizes of the angles.

Painting _____

Figure A _____

Figure B _____

Figure C _____

Figure D _____

Part B If Samir combined figure B and figure C, what type of figure would he form? Explain.

_____

_____

_____

_____

Lines of Symmetry

4.G.3

A figure is **symmetric** when it can be folded to make matching halves.

Congruent figures are the same shape and the same size. They do **not** have to be in the same position.

A **line of symmetry** is a line that can be drawn through a figure to divide it into **congruent** halves. The halves are congruent because they are mirror images of each other.

Which figure has a line of symmetry?

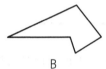

A   B

Figure A can be folded along a vertical, or up and down, line to make matching halves. Figure A has a line of symmetry.

There is no way to draw a line on figure B to divide it into matching halves. Figure B does not have a line of symmetry.

Some figures have more than one line of symmetry. They can be divided in more than one way to make congruent halves.

How many lines of symmetry does this figure have?

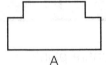

Horizontal lines go across.

This shape can be folded along a horizontal line to make matching halves.

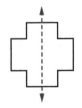

Vertical lines go up and down.

This shape can be folded along a vertical line to make matching halves.

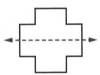

Diagonal lines go at a slant.

This shape can be folded along diagonal lines to make matching halves.

This shape has four lines of symmetry.

SAMPLE How many lines of symmetry does the figure here have?

A zero   **B** one   **C** two   **D** three

The correct answer is C. The figure has two lines of symmetry.

A vertical line divides the figure into congruent triangles:  .

A horizontal line divides the figure in matching halves: .

1 Which of the following correctly shows the line or lines of symmetry for the figure?

A   **C**

B   **D**

2 How many lines of symmetry does the figure below have?

A zero   **C** three

B two   **D** four

3 Which of the following figures does **not** have a line of symmetry?

A   **C**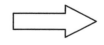

B   **D**

4 How many lines of symmetry does the figure below have?

A zero   **C** two

B one   **D** four

5 Which of the following figures has exactly two lines of symmetry?

A   **C**

B   **D**

6 Which of these figures has the fewest lines of symmetry?

A 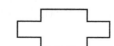   **C**

B   **D**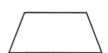

SAMPLE How many lines of symmetry
does this butterfly have?

Answer _____

 The butterfly has one line of symmetry.
A vertical line of symmetry divides the
butterfly into matching halves:

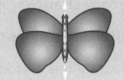

7 This diagram shows a bird's eye view of the Pentagon Building in
Washington, D.C. Draw the lines of symmetry on the building.
How many lines of symmetry does this figure have?

Answer _____

8 Kara says she drew all the lines of
symmetry on this square. Is she
correct? Explain.

_____

_____

_____

9 Luke drew these pictures of a star and the moon.

Draw all the lines of symmetry on the star and the moon. How many
lines of symmetry does each shape have?

Star _____ **Moon** _____

10 Look at the letters of the alphabet below.

A B C D E F G H I J K L M
N O P Q R S T U V W X Y Z

Part A Write four letters that have at least one line of symmetry. Explain why they are symmetric.

Which letters look the same left and right? Which letters look the same top and bottom?

_____

_____

_____

Part B Write four letters that do **not** have a line of symmetry. Explain why they are not symmetric.

_____

_____

_____

11 Petra wants to cut a shape out of paper. She wants the shape to have eight sides and to be symmetrical.

Part A In the space below, draw a shape that Petra could cut out.

Part B After Petra cuts out the shape, she folds it on the line of symmetry. Explain how Petra knows what the line of symmetry is.

_____

_____

_____

REVIEW

Geometry

Read each problem. Circle the letter of the best answer.

1 Which of the following shows a pair of perpendicular rays?

2 How can you classify this triangle based on its angles?

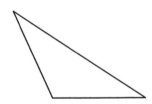

A obtuse triangle   **C** acute triangle

B right triangle   **D** straight triangle

3 How many lines of symmetry does this figure have?

A zero   **C** two

B one   **D** four

4 Shauna drew an angle that measured 38°. What kind of angle did Shauna draw?

A straight   **C** acute

B obtuse   **D** right

5 Which of these shows line *QR*?

6 Which of these is **not** a parallelogram?

7 What is the measure of this angle? Use your protractor.

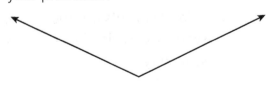

A 40°   **C** 130°

B 50°   **D** 140°

8 What are four ways to classify this figure?

Answer _____

9 In the space at the right, draw an angle formed by $\overrightarrow{QP}$ and $\overrightarrow{QR}$.

What is the name of this angle?

Answer _____

10 Look at the figure at the right. Angle *WXY* measures 85°. Angle *YXZ* measures 40°. What is the measure of angle *WXZ*? Explain.

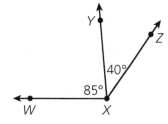

_____

_____

11 Draw a pair of parallel lines below.

Explain how you know they are parallel lines.

_____

_____

12 Draw all the lines of symmetry for this figure.

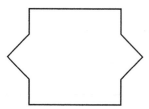

13 Janelle drew a rectangle with a triangle inside it.

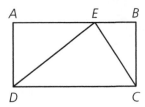

Part A Classify the following figures formed by Janelle's drawing.

Figure EBC _____   **Figure EBCD** _____

Figure EDC _____

Part B What type of angle is ∠EDA? Explain your answer.

_____

_____

14 Use your protractor to help you answer this question.

Part A In the space below, draw ∠EFG so that it measures 60°.

Part B Angle EFG and ∠HFE share ray FE. Angle HFG measures 120°. Draw ray FH on your figure above to make ∠HFG. Explain how you can find the measure of ∠HFE.

_____

_____

_____

_____

PRACTICE TEST

Read each problem. Circle the letter of the best answer.

1 Find the sum.

$$17{,}658$$
$$+32{,}951$$

A 49,609   **C** 50,609

B 50,509   **D** 51,609

2 Which fraction is equivalent to the shaded part of this model?

A $\frac{3}{10}$ **C** $\frac{1}{3}$

B $\frac{8}{16}$ **D** $\frac{9}{24}$

3 The population of Stratton is 17,089. Which digit in 17,089 has the greatest value?

A 1   **C** 8

B 7   **D** 9

4 What is the rule?

96, 48, 24, 12, 6, 3

A subtract 48   **C** multiply by 2

B subtract 42   **D** divide by 2

5 Arnold has $\frac{70}{100}$ kilogram of oatmeal. Which fraction is equivalent to $\frac{70}{100}$?

A $\frac{1}{7}$ **C** $\frac{7}{1}$

B $\frac{10}{70}$ **D** $\frac{7}{10}$

6 How many lines of symmetry does this figure have?

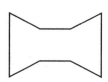

A zero   **C** four

B two   **D** five

7 The length of a rectangle is 16 cm. Its width is 7 cm. What is its perimeter?

A 23 cm   **C** 46 cm

B 39 cm   **D** 112 cm

8 Which inequality is true?

A 10,492 > 10,942

B 43,210 < 34,021

C 28,571 > 25,758

D 15,839 < 13,589

9 What is the measure of this angle? Use your protractor.

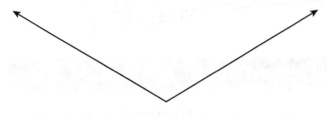

A   50°

B   60°

C   120°

D   130°

10 Hank lives more than $\frac{3}{4}$ mile from his school. Which fraction is greater than $\frac{3}{4}$?

A $\frac{5}{6}$

C $\frac{5}{8}$

B $\frac{9}{12}$

D $\frac{3}{5}$

11 A speedboat costs $43,752. What is $43,752 rounded to the nearest thousand?

A $43,800

C $44,000

B $43,000

D $45,000

12 Kelly, Hamid, and Garth sell raffle tickets. Kelly sells 65 tickets and Hamid sells 52 tickets. If the three friends sell 186 tickets in all, how many tickets does Garth sell?

A   69

C   117

B   79

D   121

13 Lara is covering the top of a rectangular table with tiles. She uses 72 tiles in 9 equal rows. Which equation could she solve to find how many tiles are in each row?

A $72 - n = 9$

C $72 \times 9 = n$

B $9 \times n = 72$

D $9 \div n = 72$

14 Which names an angle in this figure?

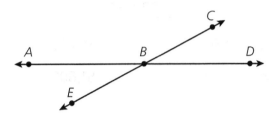

A $\overline{AD}$

C $\angle ACD$

B $\overrightarrow{BC}$

D $\angle EBD$

15 Which fraction is equal to the decimal marked by an arrow on the number line?

0.11

A $\frac{1}{11}$

C $\frac{11}{11}$

B $\frac{11}{100}$

D $\frac{11}{1}$

16 Find the difference.

$$\frac{11}{12} - \frac{3}{12} = \square$$

A $\frac{3}{4}$

C $\frac{8}{0}$

B $\frac{8}{12}$

D   8

Practice Test

17 Which is equal to 12,000 g?

  A 1,200 kg   **C** 12 kg

  B 120 kg   **D** 1.2 kg

18 Which shape is **not** a parallelogram?

  A trapezoid   **C** rectangle

  B square   **D** rhombus

19 Divide:

$$8\overline{)632}$$

  A 77   **C** 79

  B 78   **D** 89

20 What is the difference in length between the longest and shortest toy cars?

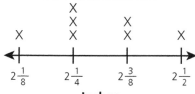

TOY CAR LENGTHS

Inches

  A $\frac{1}{8}$ in.   **C** $\frac{3}{8}$ in.

  B $\frac{1}{2}$ in.   **D** $1\frac{3}{8}$ in.

21 Which statement about parallel lines is true?

  A They are found in right triangles.

  B They never meet.

  C They are also called perpendicular lines.

  D They form a 90° angle where they intersect.

22 Which is **not** a multiple of 3?

  A 21   **C** 54

  B 29   **D** 72

23 What is $\frac{5}{8} + \frac{2}{8}$?

  A $\frac{3}{8}$ **C** $\frac{7}{8}$

  B $\frac{3}{4}$ **D** 7

24 Which two shapes come next?

▲▷▼◁▲▷▼◁▲ _?_ , _?_

  A ◀△

  B △▶

  C ▶△

  D ▷▼

25 Solve:

$$5\frac{3}{4} - 3\frac{1}{4} = \square$$

  A $2\frac{2}{4}$ **C** $3\frac{1}{2}$

  B $2\frac{3}{4}$ **D** 9

26 Frieda spent $\frac{3}{12}$ of a day helping at her grandfather's store. She spent $\frac{2}{12}$ of a day at the pool. What fraction of the day did Frieda spend doing these two things?

  A $\frac{1}{12}$ **C** $\frac{5}{12}$

  B $\frac{1}{3}$ **D** $\frac{3}{4}$

27 Omar's turtle weighs more than 0.45 kg but less than 0.5 kg. Which could be the weight of the turtle?

A 0.4 kg   **C** 0.5 kg

B 0.47 kg   **D** 0.51 kg

28 A video store received a shipment of b DVDs on Monday. On Wednesday, the store received a shipment of 45 DVDs. This number was 5 times the size of the shipment on Monday. Which number sentence shows this?

A $5 \times b = 45$ **C** $b + 5 = 45$

B $45 \times b = 5$ **D** $45 + 5 = b$

29 What fraction of a circle is equal to an angle of 90°?

A $\frac{1}{2}$ **C** $\frac{1}{4}$

B $\frac{1}{3}$ **D** $\frac{3}{4}$

30 A rectangle has an area of 42 cm². Which could be the measures of its length and width?

A 17 cm, 4 cm

B 7 cm, 6 cm

C 42 cm, 4 cm

D 40 cm, 2 cm

31 Find the difference of 7,004 − 726. Show your work.

Answer _____

32 The bowling alley is $\frac{62}{100}$ kilometer from Regina's house. The
skateboard park is $\frac{2}{10}$ kilometer directly beyond the bowling alley.
What is the total distance from Regina's house to the skateboard park?
Explain how you found the total distance.

_____

_____

_____

_____

33 How many degrees need to be added to this angle in order for it to
form a right angle? Use your protractor.

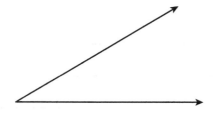

Answer _____

34 A farmer has 42 small fruit trees to plant in even rows. Use factor pairs
to find how many trees the farmer can plant in equal rows. Name all
the possible ways.

_____

_____

_____

35 Fabian finished a race in 3 minutes 5 seconds. Ling finished the same race in 190 seconds. Who was the first to finish the race? By how many seconds did the winner win? Explain.

_____

_____

_____

36 Which numbers from 55 to 60 are prime and which are composite? Explain how you know your answers are correct.

_____

_____

_____

37 How is a square like a rectangle? How is it different? Explain.

_____

_____

_____

38 Explain why the quotient of 560 ÷ 5 has three digits but the quotient of 560 ÷ 8 has only two digits.

_____

_____

_____

39 If a chicken can lay 250 eggs in one year, how many eggs can it lay in 3 years? Write and solve a number sentence to show this.

Answer _____

40 Von makes and sells vases. He has 413 vases in stock. He sells 195 vases at a crafts fair. Then he makes 108 more vases. Von calculates that he has 515 vases in stock now. Is Von's answer reasonable? Use rounding to estimate the answer. If Von's answer is not reasonable, find the actual answer.

_____

_____

_____

41 Praveena has a microscope that is $\frac{44}{100}$ meter long. The microscope case is $\frac{5}{10}$ meter long. Write the decimal notation for each measure. Then mark and label the decimals on the number line below.

Answer _____

42 Bret buys 0.52 kilogram of cherries, 0.75 liter of orange juice, and 0.3 kilogram of grapes. Which of these measures cannot be compared with the others? Explain why.

_____

_____

43 Shaquille surveyed his class to find out how many dogs each student has. The results are shown in the table below.

Number of Dogs	Fraction of Class
0	$\frac{1}{2}$
1	$\frac{3}{12}$
2	$\frac{1}{12}$
3 or more	$\frac{2}{12}$

What fraction of students in Shaquille's class has 1 or more dogs? Show your work.

Answer _____

44 An animal pen is a rectangle 15 yards long and 3 yards wide. Tristan increases the length by 5 yards and the width by 2 yards. What is the area of the new animal pen?

Answer _____

45 Bus A takes $\frac{3}{4}$ hour to get from the mall to Shana's house. Bus B takes $\frac{7}{12}$ hour to go from the mall to Shana's house. Which bus takes less time? Write equivalent fractions to compare the numbers. Show your work.

Answer _____

46 Norton believes that $\frac{5}{6}$ is the same as both $5 \times \frac{1}{6}$ and $\frac{1}{6} + \frac{1}{6} + \frac{1}{6} + \frac{1}{6} + \frac{1}{6}$. Is he correct? Draw a model to prove your answer.

Answer _____

47 In the space below, draw line *AB*. Then draw ray *BC* perpendicular to line *AB*. Finally draw line segment *CA*.

48 At the beginning of track season, Henri's best long jump was $22\frac{5}{6}$ feet. By the end of the season, he had jumped $25\frac{1}{6}$ ft. How much farther could Henri jump at the end of the season? Show your work.

Answer _____

49 Taylor found this leaf in her backyard.

Taylor says that the leaf has a line of symmetry. Is she correct? Explain.

_____

_____

_____

50 The rule for a pattern is "add 5." The pattern starts with the number 8. Find the first six numbers in this pattern. What is true about all the numbers in this pattern?

_____

_____

_____

Read each problem. Write your answer to each part.

51 Javonne multiplied 78 × 69. His work and the product he found are shown below.

$$\begin{array}{r} 69 \\ \times 78 \\ \hline 552 \\ 4\,230 \\ \hline 4{,}782 \end{array}$$

Part A What mistake did Javonne make?

____

____

____

Part B Find the correct product. Show your work.

Answer ______________________

52 Dita and Eric take music lessons. Dita has a $\frac{1}{2}$-hour lesson twice a week. Eric has a $\frac{3}{4}$-hour lesson once a week.

Part A How many total hours does Dita spend at lessons in a month of 4 weeks? Show your work.

Answer ____________

Part B Who spends more time at lessons in 4 weeks, Eric or Dita? Explain.

____

____

53 Kayla wants to put up a mesh fence around her garden to keep out rabbits. She drew a diagram of her garden below.

```
┌─────────────────────┐
│                     │
│                     │
│                     │
│   Garden        4 yd│
│                     │
│                     │
│                     │
└─────────────────────┘
         5 yd
```

Part A How many feet of fencing does Kayla need to go around the entire garden? Explain how you found your answer.

_____

_____

_____

_____

Part B The garden store sells 25-foot rolls of fencing for $21. How much money will Kayla spend to fence her garden? Explain.

_____

_____

_____

GLOSSARY

acute angle — an angle that measures less than 90°

acute triangle — a triangle with three acute angles

addend — numbers that are added in an addition problem to find a sum

align — to line up

alternate — to arrange in order by turns

angle — a figure formed by two rays that share an endpoint and extend in different directions

area — the amount of space inside a figure, measured in square units. The area formula for a rectangle is Area = length × width.

area model — a rectangular model divided into rows

array — a model using rows and columns of symbols or shapes

associative property — allows grouping of numbers with parentheses to be added or multiplied: $a + (b + c) = (a + b) + c$ and $a \times (b \times c) = (a \times b) \times c$

capacity — the measure of how much liquid something holds

common denominator — a number that is a multiple of every denominator of the fractions in a set

commutative property — allows numbers to be added or multiplied in any order: $a + b = b + a$ and $a \times b = b \times a$

compare — to decide which of two numbers is greater in value

composite number — a whole number that has more than two factors

congruent — equal in length, measure, or shape

convert — to change from one unit of measurement to another

customary system — a system of measurement used in the United States. It includes units of
- length—inch, foot, yard, mile
- capacity—fluid ounce, cup, pint, quart, gallon
- weight— ounce, pound, ton

D

data	information in the form of numbers
decimal notation	a way to write a fraction with a denominator of 10 or 100 using place values
degree	a unit of angle measure; a unit of temperature measure
denominator	the number of parts in the whole or set, the number on the bottom of a fraction
diagonal	slanted
difference	the answer in a subtraction problem
dimensions	the length and width of a plane figure
dividend	the number being divided in a division problem
divisor	the number doing the dividing in a division problem
dot plot	a line plot

E

endpoint	a point marking the end of a line segment or ray
equation	a number sentence that says two expressions are equal
equivalent fractions	two or more fractions that represent the same value
estimation	a way to find a value that is close but not exact. Estimation strategies include

- **rounding**—using rounded numbers to add, subtract, multiply, or divide
- **front-end estimation**—using only the first digit or digits of a number to add, subtract, multiply, or divide
- **compatible numbers**—using nearby numbers that are easy to work with to carry out operations

expanded form	a way to write a number that shows the number as the sum of the values of its places
express	to write
expression	a grouping of numbers and operations that shows the value of something

 **factor pair**   any two whole numbers that are multiplied to get a product

factors   whole numbers that multiply to form a product

formula   an equation that states a rule

 horizontal   across

 improper fraction   a fraction in which the numerator is equal to or greater than the denominator

inequality   a number sentence that compares two numbers

inverse operations   operations that undo each other, opposite operations. Addition and subtraction are inverse operations. Multiplication and division are inverse operations.

 key words   words that indicate operations

 length   a measure of how long something is

like denominators   the same denominators

line   a figure made up of points that extends forever in both directions

line of symmetry   a line that can be drawn through a figure to divide it into congruent halves

line plot   a plot in which data is represented by X's placed over a number line. Also called a dot plot.

line segment   a piece of a line; its ends are marked by endpoints

lowest terms   the simplest form of a fraction in which the terms cannot be divided by a number other than 1

mass a measure of how heavy something is in metric units

mental math a way to do operations in your head. Mental math strategies include

- **breaking apart**—to break a number into a sum of two addends to make it easier to combine with another number
- **compensation**— to add to a number to make 10 to make it easy to add, and then to subtract the added number from the sum
- **patterns**—to use patterns of zeros to find products and quotients

metric system a system of measurement used in most of the world. It includes units of

- length— millimeter, centimeter, meter, kilometer
- capacity—milliliter, liter
- mass— gram, kilogram

mixed number a whole number plus a fraction

multiples the products of a number and nonzero whole numbers

number pattern an ordered set of numbers that is generated by a rule

numerator the number of parts talked about, the number on the top of fraction

obtuse angle an angle that measures more than 90° but less than 180°

obtuse triangle a triangle with one obtuse angle

order to arrange numbers by value from least to greatest or greatest to least

parallel lines lines that are always the same distance apart and never touch

parallelogram a quadrilateral with two pairs of parallel sides

pattern a sequence or design that repeats or grows according to a rule

perimeter the distance around a figure

perpendicular lines lines that meet at a right angle

place value the value given to the place a digit has in a number; each place has a value 10 times greater than the place to its right.

hundred millions	ten millions	millions	hundred thousands	ten thousands	thousands	hundreds	tens	ones	tenths	hundredths
4	5	6,	7	8	9,	0	1	2	.3	4

point a fixed location in space

polygon a two-dimensional figure with line segments for sides

prime number a whole number that has exactly two factors, 1 and itself

product the answer in a multiplication problem

protractor a tool used to measure the size of an angle

quadrilateral a polygon with four sides

quotient the answer in a division problem

R ray — a figure that has one endpoint and extends forever in the other direction

rectangle — a parallelogram with four right angles

regroup — to exchange 1 in one place for 10 in the place to its right, or 10 in one place for 1 in the place to its left; example: 2 tens can be regrouped as 1 ten and 10 ones

rhombus — a parallelogram with four equal sides

right angle — an angle that measures 90°

right triangle — a triangle with one right angle

round — to replace a number with a close number that tells about how many or how much

S sequence — the order of something

shape pattern — a pattern that is made up of shapes

square — a rectangle with four equal sides

square unit — a unit of measure for area that is 1 unit long and 1 unit wide, such as square inches, square centimeters, or square meters

standard form — a number written as the sum of the values of its places

straight angle — an angle that measures exactly 180°; forms a straight line

sum — the answer in an addition problem

symmetric — able to be divided into matching halves

T terms — the numerator and denominator of a fraction

trapezoid — a quadrilateral with exactly one pair of parallel sides

triangle — a polygon with three sides

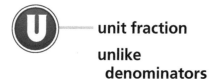 **unit fraction**   a fraction with a numerator of 1

unlike   different denominators
  denominators

 **variable**   a symbol or letter that stands for a value that is
  unknown or can change

vertex   the endpoint shared by the two rays that form an angle

vertical   up and down

 **weight**   a measure of how heavy something is in customary units

word form   a number name written in words